All My Funny Ones

A Collection of Short Stories

Mindy Littman Holland

DEDICATION

I dedicate this book to my husband, Grant,
who has been making me laugh since 1987.

CONTENTS

ACKNOWLEDGMENTS

To my husband, Grant, thank you for being a wonderful editor and my greatest fan. And, to all the people who have read my books and blogs over the years, thank you for your very valuable feedback and for continuing to read me. You make writing a joy for me.

HAPPY NEW YEAR 2012

A new year has begun, full of the usual mystery, apprehension and promise that new years bring. As each year passes, I think about what has been most consistent in my life. The answer to that is I have consistently been enthralled by the people with whom I have crossed paths; people whom I have loved, people with whom I have worked, people with whom I have traveled, people who have made me laugh and people who have broken my heart.
I am interested in all that makes us human – our complexity, our eccentricity and our vulnerability. My stories are about people who have touched me in big and small ways and have made a lasting impression on my soul. In the coming months, I will be sharing these stories with you.
Happy reading!

DANCING WITH DIEGO

JANUARY 2012

Diego was never that easy to get along with. He was an irascible Spaniard from Argentina who looked like an escapee from a 1930's mobster movie. He wore pinstriped suits with enormous shoulder pads and his starched white shirts were monogrammed with cursive initials. He was old-fashioned enough to wear heavy gold cufflinks and tiepins, but modern enough to have a wife who smoked pot once or twice. He didn't like to be seen with people who weren't well put together.

So, when we were traveling around the country on a two-week press tour and I managed to catch the flu somewhere between Boston and San Jose as we sat at the back of a plane populated by nervous smokers, Diego decided I was too ugly to travel with.

"What's the matter with you, woman, you look like shit," he said, as I

1

gazed at him through feverish eyes. "Comb your hair, or something."

Actually, we nearly missed that flight altogether. We got stuck in heavy traffic in front of the Callahan Tunnel on our way to Logan Airport.

"What the hell are all these people doing here?" I asked.

Diego said, "Why don't you take a poll, lady? Go from car to car. Tell people to roll their windows down and ask, "Hey, what the FUCK are you doing here?"

I didn't take him up on it.

Fortunately, it was the last leg of our trip – we only had another meeting or two to go on the west coast. If I died en route, he would probably be able to wing the rest. I turned my head away and wondered how I was going to make it all the way across the country with a fever of one hundred and three. Diego had gotten sick in the middle of the trip and hadn't looked too hot himself. In fact, I got sick nursing him. Now, the son of a bitch wanted to trade me in for a prettier PR rep.

When the plane touched down for a stopover in Dallas, Diego wanted to leave me there altogether. By that time, my fever was bursting out of my eyeballs. I probably wouldn't have been able to find my way to a hotel, so I covered my face with my collar and followed him, like an out-of-favor Geisha, to our next flight.

The next morning, he asked a couple of business associates to carry me back to Atlanta – and "carry" was the operative word. I was down and out for the next seven weeks.

It wasn't the first time we parted ways mid-trip. The very first time I went on a press tour, I didn't have the foggiest idea of what I was doing. Since Diego was my boss, I asked him what I was supposed to do. In typical Diego fashion, he squiggled a Mont Blanc pen in the air and said, "Oh, lady, you know."

Actually, I didn't. I set up several appointments with publishers in the Northeast. I had nothing – no story, no news, nothing. I really had no idea of what I was doing – so I resorted to thanking publishers for carrying our ads.

The publisher of one trade rag in Hasbrouck Heights looked at me like he thought I was cranking his chain and said, "You don't thank us for carrying your ads, darling – you pay us big money for that – *we* thank *you*."

Well – at least he taught me something. After a few days of shambling around on my own, Diego came flying in, took off with my rental car and stranded me with a co-worker at a Sheraton, with instructions for the co-worker to get me back to the airport. The associate wasn't too thrilled about having to take me to Newark. I may have had to sleep with him. What the hell, it was the eighties. If it were the nineties, I probably would've called a cab.

Another time, Diego and I were staying at the Dorset Hotel in

Rockefeller Center. By that time, I knew exactly what I was doing and had arranged meetings with editors all over New York. Unfortunately, a hurricane was predicted and that closed the whole city down. Diego had already confiscated my room, which had a queen-sized bed in it, and left me his room, which sported two thin twin beds with apple green bedspreads. He got bored waiting for the hurricane and decided to walk to the Waldorf and look at prostitutes.

At three o'clock that morning, I got a phone call. I squinted at the clock and picked up the phone. It was Diego. "Hey, lady," he said. "You want to go dancing?"

"Have you lost your mind? I was sleeping – we have meetings in the morning. Besides, where can you even go dancing at this hour?"

"At the Rainbow Room, lady. Just don't tell my wife. She'll cut my balls off."

Nancy would have, too. I could picture her with a cleaver.

I actually went dancing with him that night at the Rainbow Room. We danced well together but he got a hard-on every time we hit the floor.

"What the hell is that?" I would ask, pointing.

"Don't call attention to it, lady," Diego would mutter, clearing his throat and pulling me closer.

I didn't take offense. It was just one of those things. Truly.

It wasn't the only place we danced. I remember the night we glided around F. Scott's in Georgetown. I was wearing a furry sapphire sweater, which had covered his fancy suit in fuzzy little blue balls as we danced cheek to cheek. While we said goodnight at my door, I extracted a lint brush from my purse and gave him the brush-off before he headed to his room – just in case he needed that suit in the morning.

We also danced at a company Christmas party at the Peachtree Plaza. It was a very elegant party. He was in a tux and his wife was in a sequined evening gown. All I remember was dancing with him and pointing down. He muttered, "Ignore it, lady." Fortunately, it was a dark room.

I remember when Diego was general manager of a joint venture partnership with a west coast-based company. He hired a man from Plains, Georgia to manage the project. The man's name was Floyd and he was a remarkably sweet guy.

I was out at the Stage Deli in New York with Floyd when he ordered a corned beef sandwich on white bread with butter and a glass of milk. The waitress, who was wearing orange lipstick up to her nostrils, grimaced and said, "Oh, no, darling, I won't get you that."

I felt like pelting the waitress with matzo balls but Floyd just smiled and smiled. I told him to let me order for him.

Hey, when I'm in Plains, he can order ham hocks and red-eye gravy for me. Coming to think of it, Floyd was one of the people Diego enlisted to take my sick ass home from San Jose. He was a wonderful man and, like Diego, he, too, became CEO of many a company. And, like Diego and I, we clocked plenty of time on the road together. But, unlike Diego and I, we never tangoed together at the Rainbow Room under a mirror ball in the middle of the night.

Diego did me a kindness early on in our travels. It was so long ago I was still living in a condominium. Diego was going to carry my bag to my door when we returned from a trip. Just as he was removing my suitcase from his trunk I spotted my cat hunkered down under a bush.

"Come, pussy brains," I cooed.

Diego didn't see the cat. He dropped the bag in a huff and said, "How can you call me pussy brains? Don't you have any respect, woman? Carry your own damn luggage."

Diego ended up moving to Seattle to become the CEO of a company there. While on a fishing trip in Destin, he caught a cold and then developed an arrhythmia. The doctors put him on Coumadin and it gave him a big cerebral hemorrhage that nearly killed him. He was forty-two. Eventually, he had to move back to Atlanta, where his wife's business was based. He had a young son by then. I spent years helping him with his speech and reading skills, but I didn't really do him much good – at least, his language didn't improve. He was still able to swear like a champ, though.

And, one day, he pointed out that even though he was half blind and half paralyzed and couldn't speak, his dick still worked perfectly. I was tempted to ask him to dance, but restrained myself. Our dancing days were over. And, Diego's working days were over. So, when we weren't working on reading and speech, we went to the movies.

One time we went to see a movie that was supposed to be kind of racy. "Don't tell Nancy", he wrote on a napkin. We had stopped to get a lame hotdog before the movie – that's where the napkin came from. There was one sex scene at the beginning of the movie and it was over within ten seconds. Diego didn't find this too satisfying. He lifted his un-paralyzed left hand, looked at me with exasperation and yelled, "Well?" That became a lifelong family gesture – I may have told him that once or twice.

Diego died of a massive stroke at sixty. He lived long enough to see his son grow up. His marriage didn't make it, but neither did his first two. He was living with a woman who loved him at the time and he still traveled plenty. He still couldn't speak, but he was able to sing a little. He always loved to sing.

At the end of every conversation we ever had, he told me that he loved me. And, when I see him in my thoughts, he's always smiling. The Rainbow Room has gone out of business, but how nice it would be to go dancing again in the middle of the night. Well?

A TRIBUTE TO MY FATHER

Before my father passed away in October 2011, he told me that one of the greatest things he ever did was take the family on a road trip out west. It was just before my older brother left home to go to college. And, what a trip it was. Today would have been my father's eighty-seventh birthday. Dad, thank you for giving me wonderful memories to cherish. Someday, we will hit the road with each other again. Happy birthday. I love you.

SCREAMING ACROSS AMERICA

JANUARY 2012

When it comes to family vacations, Chevy Chase (aka Clark Griswold) has nothing on my father. Just before my older brother, Alan, left home to start college, our dad woke us at two in the morning and told us to grab our shorts and toothbrushes because we were heading west. I really don't recall getting much more notice than that before we hit the road in the dead of night. It was 1967 and I was fourteen.

We started out in New York and woke up in South Bend, Indiana. Not only were we heading west, we were hauling ass across the country like we were escaping from Godzilla. My father was driving like a madman.

Nothing was going on in South Bend. Alan was the only other driver in the car and he took over the driving there so my father could get some sleep. My father directed him to just stay on Route 80 until he awoke – or until he hit something.

I know there was a driver change in Sioux City, Iowa because Alan was no longer in the driver seat. He was in the back seat with me when he suddenly started screaming and flailing his limbs like he was on fire. My father swerved all over the road and damn near killed the whole family.

What happened was that in Sioux City, we had stopped in some tourist trap with a teepee and some antlers and other artifacts. After Alan and I crawled out of the teepee, he tried on the antlers. What we didn't know until we were down the road was that Alan had picked up a boarder, either from the teepee or the antlers. He suddenly felt eyes staring at him and discovered a praying mantis on his shoulder the size of a 747. With the way Alan carried on, you would've thought a tarantula had draped a hairy leg around his neck.

When Alan started screaming, we all started screaming. I suspect the praying mantis was also screaming. The poor thing finally flew out the window, where it held on to the glass of the fishtailing Buick for dear life until it just blew away. It was the first of many screams on our trip west. We sat on the side of the road for a few minutes gasping and checking each other's vital signs before moving on.

We headed into the Black Hills of South Dakota and marveled at Mount Rushmore without considering how the Lakota Sioux felt about having a bunch of pasty-faced white guys carved into one of their sacred mountains. We went to Yellowstone Park and timed Old Faithful (which I thought of as "Whole Face Full"), oohed and aahed at bubbling sulfur springs and tried to keep from getting eaten by bears. We went to a rodeo and ate barbecued bison in Cheyenne and visited Cody, where old coots in cowboy costumes shot it out in the dusty middle of town with blanks. Yee-haw.

By the time we were going through the Grand Tetons en route to Jackson Hole, we were all ready to shoot each other. I think we were sleep-deprived from fighting bedbugs in the fleabag motels we were staying in. Plus, my mother was chain-smoking back then and wouldn't let us lower the car windows because her hair might stir. And, she was taking a two-and-a-half-week vacation from showering because the water in all the fleabags smelled of sulfur.

Alan and I were irritating each other in the back seat and finally, my formerly unflappable father lost it. He announced that he was going to take out the whole family and floored the gas pedal. The G-force wrapped our cheeks around our ears as we drove through the high sierra at a hundred miles an hour. It's a little hard to scream with your cheeks wrapped around your ears, but we gave it our best shot. And, we made it to Jackson Hole in about ten minutes.

There were spectacular mountains and scenery all around us. My mother kept remarking, "If you've seen one mountain, you've seen them all." Then, we'd get to a new range and she'd change her tune for about a minute. And, speaking of tunes, my father couldn't tolerate the sound of silence. If the car got too quiet, he either whistled a mazurka or quacked like a duck. He read license plates aloud. He had one-sided conversations with other motorists – all of whom he claimed to recognize from somewhere. Hey, it was all part of the ride. We were all babbling to ourselves after a while. But, only my father quacked.

We headed toward the Grand Canyon and that was such an amazing sight. My father told us that he had an overwhelming urge to jump, which would've left us short one driver. It was a good thing he stuck around because he got some good shots of my brother and I trying to hurl my mother over the edge while she made Three Stooges noises. It was one of the few times during the trip when there was actually film in the camera.

We drove across the Mohave Desert in the middle of the night to keep the car from overheating. And, we stopped in Needles in the daytime, just to hear people say, "Is it hot enough for you?" It was four hundred degrees in Needles. I felt like saying, "No, it's not quite hot enough. We were counting on being vaporized."

We went to Disneyland in Anaheim. I don't remember going on any rides, but I do recall Mickey Mouse trying to strangle my brother. That was worth the price of admission — seeing some doofus in a mouse head and red pants with his white-gloved mitts wrapped around my brother's throat. I wish my father had gotten a picture of that!

We went down to San Diego to visit with my father's Aunt Rose and her husband, Ted. They had a beautiful home on the edge of the Pacific. Alan and I got to share a room and, every morning, at around five a.m., Aunt Rose would poke her head in and cheerily sing, "Goood morrrrrningggg." I can't imagine that she woke my parents up that way. My mother needed her twelve hours of sleep at night. What the hell was Aunt Rose doing up at that hour? It wasn't like they had cows to milk. They owned a tobacco shop, for Christ's sake.

We stayed at the Flamingo Hotel on the Las Vegas Strip. Alan, at eighteen, looked fourteen; and I, at fourteen, looked twenty-five. Back then, you got dressed up at night in Vegas and, in an evening gown, I had no trouble getting into the casinos. On the other hand, my parents were threatened with a fine if they didn't get my big brother the hell out of there.

Maybe I should've gone to a baccarat table and smoked a cigarette out of a long holder because, while I was impressed with the vastness and beauty of America, I was mostly interested in impressing herds of roaming American boys. Of course, there weren't a whole lot of boys in dinner jackets playing roulette so I didn't meet anybody. Alan was a serious horn dog himself. He must've felt up every female statue at Caesar's Palace.

It was hotter than blazing hell in Vegas in July so we played in the pool like the children we actually were and went with our parents to see Ann-Margret perform at the Riviera Hotel. We had a wholesome time of it, in spite of the abundance of topless ladies and sleazy yahoos who came out of the hills to gamble and drink themselves to death in the neon desert.

We went to the Petrified Forest. There were signs posted all over the place, warning people not to take any wood with them when they left. My mother slipped a few pieces into her bra and said, "Let them search me." Alan and I were horrified. We thought our mother was going to get arrested and have to serve time in the middle of rural Arizona. On the other hand, we weren't going to lose a driver and she still hadn't showered. Hmmm.

She didn't get caught and, somehow, I ended up with the pieces of petrified wood. Forty years later, I performed a ritual. When my husband and I visited the Petrified Forest in 2007, I smuggled the wood back in my cleavage and ceremoniously returned the pieces of wood to their mother rock. I actually found a perfect match right near the visitor center. It made sense. My family wasn't very adventurous – in fact, we probably didn't venture further than twenty feet away from our car the whole trip.

We got stuck in a sandstorm in the Painted Desert. Turns out, there's always a sandstorm going on in the Painted Desert.

We almost died trying to cross a street to get to a Chinese restaurant in St. Louis, Missouri. I don't think there was a single traffic light in St. Louis, back then – just an arch – and a lot of good that did us.

We kind of dozed for a few states – even my father, who was driving. There are some dull-ass states out there.

On the last night of our trip, we ended up in a parking lot in Wheeling, West Virginia. It was time to look for a motel, but my parents made an executive decision – we would sleep in the car. At least, there wouldn't be any bedbugs to keep us awake. I finally got to sit in the driver's seat, where I had to try to sleep with a steering wheel shoved into my forehead. We woke up next to a truck full of pigs. At least, we couldn't smell my mother anymore. Of course, the rest of us smelled like sulfur. The pigs looked dismayed.

And, then, as if by magic, we were back where we started from two-and-a half weeks before. Alan left for Penn State shortly thereafter and I left for Brandeis four years later and we never took an extended family trip again. My father remembered it as the best trip he ever took – and that included his journey into Europe during WWII, to liberate concentration camps. My mother still can't distinguish one mountain from another – but she returned to Las Vegas with my father thirty-seven times over the years (and once with the whole family when they celebrated their fiftieth anniversary). My brother was the one who reminded me that it was a praying mantis on his shoulder in Sioux City rather than a tarantula. And, I have saved a couple of slivers of petrified wood, just in case my nieces want to continue the family tradition and smuggle them back into the park in their cleavage.

Chevy Chase: Eat your heart out.

WHY AM I GREEN?

Did you ever wonder about where you came from? I don't mean which city. I mean which planet. When I was a little girl, my inventive father attempted to put me to sleep with tales of our other-worldly origins. As an adult, I had reason to ask if he were actually telling me the truth. Are there any other aliens out there?

ROMULAC

MARCH 2012

If I had a nickel for every time a doctor looked at me in awe, stroked his chin and uttered, "I've never seen anything like that before," I would be able to afford two or three organ transplants by now. I am so fraught with medical anomalies the phenomenon has even transferred to my pets. For example, my vet was convinced that my cat was able to meow the alphabet. He sure as hell had never seen *that* before.

Perhaps I really was abducted when I was a kid living on Long Island. I probably have a thousand children living on Romulac right now – all wondering why they have curly black hair growing out of their enormous silver heads. Physicians all over Romulac are stroking their pointy chins right now, telepathically delivering the bad news to parents – the cosmic equivalent of "I've never seen anything like that before." Of course, to Earthlings it would sound like "bidibidibidibidibidiglarrg" – and then we would be vaporized.

I don't know if I'm actually an alien. Suffice to say, the Mayo Clinic's got a gallon of my DNA on tap – just in case they find another one of my kind in the universe. If they do, they may put us in an intergalactic zoo or try to breed us in a lab. It won't work, though. All of my eggs were poached years ago. I'm sure of it.

I was born a hell of a long time ago in a hospital in the Bronx, which is no longer there (perhaps it was carried off). At any rate, my mother's obstetrician suspected I was going to have trouble at birth because my parents had conflicting RH factors in their blood. I don't know what that means, exactly, but it has something to do with monkeys. It's a condition that doesn't affect the first child. Unfortunately, I was child number two (and I do mean that in every imaginable way). I made my pink appearance and then turned blue.

Without a complete blood transfusion, breathing was not going to be an option for me. So, my mother had to be slapped out of the ether to sign a consent form allowing the doctors to drain all of my bad blood and inject a new supply of O-positive into my umbilicus. I don't know why they couldn't have had my father sign the consent form – maybe he was out in the waiting room, working on a crossword puzzle and sucking on a toothpick. Maybe they just wanted to slap my mother. Whatever. For me it was like, "Welcome to the world. We've come to suck your blood."

And, they did. The doctors explained that the transfusion was a new procedure and they didn't know if it was going to work. So, they did what they had to do – emptied me out, filled me back up, tied a few knots and placed all six pounds of me into an intensive care unit, where I tried to adapt to the new blood supply. I'm told that I burned a very high fever while my body was screaming, "What the hell are you doing to me?" and my parents were warned that, if I pulled through, I could either be very small or mentally challenged.

My mother didn't see me for the first ten days of my life. Maybe she didn't want any bonding to take place because it would've been too hard on her if I croaked. Hey – what about me?

My father tells me he saw me right away, but it was my maternal grandmother who was the first to hold me and feed me in the ICU. If she hadn't been there, I would have bonded to the ICU nurse and spoken with a Jamaican accent.

My father told me that, in spite of having O-positive blood, the hospital wouldn't allow him to give me any. Maybe it was that bizarre bonding issue again. Who knows? All I know is I made it out of that hospital alive and I grew like a weed and taught myself to read by the time I was three. The doctor may have shrunk a few inches. I don't know. I was taller than he by the time I was nine. My mother used to say I could eat apples off his head – if he were still alive, which he wasn't.

Fast-forward a few years. Aside from a little childhood anemia (and my mother making me sick by pouring liver drippings down my throat to build up my blood – and congest my arteries), I appeared to be healthy as a horse. Unfortunately, all sorts of weird crap started going on. For example, I went through such a growth spurt at the age of eleven that I nearly went blind. (Eye chart? What eye chart?) I was also built like Sophia Loren in the sixth grade and that scared the hell out of my classmates. But, I'm getting ahead of myself.

I began to have night terrors when I was six or seven. I was afraid to sleep and I don't think it was because of the creepy Perry Mason music coming out of the TV room or my brother moaning on the other side of my bedroom wall. I was feeling a presence, and not in a good way.

My father would come into my room to try to get me to calm down. Of course, my room was dark and I couldn't see under the best of circumstances so, to me, he looked like a big gray hulk. He sat beside me on the bed and told me a story. "We are not from this place," he began.

"No?" I said. "Where are we from?"

"Have you noticed the greenish color of our skin? We are from a different world and I travel through the cosmos at night."

Holy shit. I thought we had greenish skin because we were Jews, not Martians. Was this supposed to comfort me? My own father was cruising around in space all night. No wonder he got migraines.

Then, after giving me that fabulous food for thought, he wiggled his fingers in front of my eyes like a demented hypnotist and intoned, "Sleeeeeeeeeep."

"Aaaarrrrgggggggggghhhhhhh!!!!!!!"

Years later, I had reason to call my father and ask if we actually were from a different planet.

"Why do you ask?" he said.

"Because I have a bunch of doctors walking around scratching their chins, wondering if Ashkenazi is synonymous with alien life form."

"What are you talking about?" he asked.

"Well, I have various idiopathic disorders – which means nobody knows what the hell they are – in spite of the fact that I'm healthy as a horse. So, tell me, which planet are we actually from?"

My father was at a loss for words.

I continued. "When I was very young, I crept into your bedroom one night. Mom was sound asleep and you were standing in front of your window in your boxers, looking out into the night sky. I saw yellow and red stripes in the sky beyond your body, which was standing very still. You didn't notice me and didn't seem to be mentally present. Were you traveling through the cosmos?"

There was a pause before he responded. "Of course, not," he finally said. "I was probably looking at the aurora borealis."

"Well, that explains nothing," I sighed. "Whose blood got transfused into me when I was born?"

By that time, my mother had picked up an extension. In fact, I have never had a phone conversation with my father without my mother picking up and taking over.

"What's the matter?" she asked.

"Our daughter wants to know whose blood she's got."

"From the transfusion?"

"Yeah."

"I think you got the janitor's blood," she said.

I knew she was kidding. How was she supposed to know whose blood ended up in the blood bank – probably a bunch of poor bastards who had to sell their blood for doughnuts. And, who screened blood back then?

"Was the janitor from Romulac?" I asked.

"No, I think he was from Queens."

"Well, that would explain a bad accent, but not inexplicable disorders."

"What are you talking about?" she asked.

"My doctors can't figure out what's wrong with me. On the one hand, they think I'm the healthiest specimen they've ever seen. On the other, they're wondering why I'm not dead."

That got a rise out of my mother. She started to cry, "What can they do for you?"

"Absolutely nothing. They told me to eat, drink and be merry."

I told my parents not to worry about me – that I was apparently from an indestructible race and that I was grateful to the janitor for my strange and wonderful life. I assume that I will continue to have medical anomalies for the next hundred years.

I'm going to take the doctor's advice. I'm going to eat, drink and be merry. And, I'm going to adopt a dog that sings opera.

THE BIG HIKE

Shortly after we moved to Santa Fe, New Mexico, my husband and I were invited to hike in the desert in the dead of a Rocky Mountain winter. The initial goal was to locate a herd of wild horses. As the day progressed, we eventually came up with a new goal: to locate our truck before we got eaten by mountain lions or froze to death while trying to avoid mean cowboys. Speak of lost in space!

WILD HORSE MESA

MAY 2012

I used to enjoy a good hike, usually a five-mile stroll under a canopy of trees, beside a body of flowing water. My husband, Grant, and I would pack a few nuts and a bottle of water and spend a couple of hours in the great outdoors. Every once in a while, we would spot a deer or a copperhead. One time, we ran into a goat in the middle of the Appalachian Trail. Maybe it was a satyr.

By and large, the hikes were pleasant affairs. We always got back to our car in one piece and typically followed it up with dinner and a movie. That was in Georgia where the biggest threat was possibly running into a couple of guys with banjos. Then, we moved to New Mexico.

You would think that New Mexico would be a great place to hike – and I'm sure it must be. Unfortunately, my maiden voyage was a rather turbulent one, and I don't think I will ever get over it.

It was a crisp winter day. We barely knew our neighbors across the street, but they invited us to join them on a hike on what they called Wild Horse Mesa. It wasn't actually called Wild Horse Mesa – it was a piece of desert out in the middle of the Caja del Rio Plateau – but they called it Wild Horse Mesa because they had seen wild horses there once and were determined to find them again. They said the hike would be around fifteen miles.

I said to Grant, "A fifteen-mile hike, huh – what are they, crazy?"

"It's par for the course around here," he said.

What do you take on a fifteen-mile hike – I mean, aside from an oxygen tank and flares? Who wants to take a fifteen-mile hike to see anything?

"Well, it sounds like a bit much for me," I said. "Besides," I added, "I need to prepare to leave town tomorrow." I was flying back to Atlanta in the morning. "See if they would be willing to cut the hike in half – that's the only way I can go," I said.

The neighbors, Rusty and Diane, were willing. I told them I needed to get back before dark – which sounded reasonable under any circumstance.

We headed out in the morning, taking Rusty's broken-down truck, which he rode like a bucking bronco. He was, in fact, a former rodeo bull rider. We fishtailed along for about an hour on really bumpy dirt roads, with Diane and I bouncing around in the back seat. Diane was popping ginger mints to keep from puking on Rusty's neck. There was a German shepherd, named Hercules, on a short tether in the back of the truck – and, by German shepherd I don't mean a sheepherder in lederhosen. The dog probably should've been secured under a tarp. I thought for sure we were going to hang the poor thing.

At any rate, we made it to our destination and parked the car under a tree. Trees on the Caja are all roughly five feet high and there aren't many of them. Nobody thought to bring a GPS – but Grant brought two sets of walkie-talkies. We all peed under a bush, to mark the territory, I guess, and off we went.

It was a gloriously beautiful day, full of huge blue skies and little white puffball clouds. We seemed to be the only people in the world, but there were plenty of other creatures around. We knew that because all along the way Diane was identifying droppings of various wild animals.

"That's coyote!" she exclaimed. "That's mountain lion!" "That's bear!" "That's cow!"

The only thing we didn't find was horseshit – and that's what we were really after. Because, where there's horseshit, there's usually a horse in the vicinity. And, Rusty was determined to locate a herd of wild horses – if it killed us. Hey – I'd walk a mile for a Camel, but for a horse – maybe fifteen.

A mountain loomed in front of us, all covered in snow.

"Let's climb it and have lunch," said Rusty.

I didn't want to rain on everybody's parade, but I didn't see how we could climb a mountain, have lunch, search for horseshit and still get back home in time for me to pack. I protested, but you know we ended up half-killing ourselves getting up that mountain anyway. Speak of horseshit.

The view was great, though. I think we were able to see four states and maybe a few foreign countries from up there. And then, lo and behold, we actually saw one little brown horse, all by itself in the distance, through a pair of huge binoculars. That got us all very excited. So, instead of climbing down the way we climbed up, we decided to go down another way, in pursuit of more horse sightings.

Once again, we damn near got killed slithering our way down the freaking mountain, but we made it to the bottom and proceeded to walk and walk and walk and walk and walk until we all admitted that nothing looked familiar. In fact, we could've been in Mexico. And, there weren't any horses there, either. However, we did stumble into a couple of really large cows with horns. They stared at us and wouldn't budge. Grant immediately began to walk in the opposite direction.

"Where are you going?" I asked.

Turns out, Grant's afraid of cows – especially big ones with horns. And, they didn't look like they were going to let us pass. I prepared to dive into a juniper tree, even though I'm terribly allergic to juniper berries.

"What do you suppose we should do?" I asked Rusty. Grant, in the meantime, had wandered into a different time zone.

Rusty scampered around and found a nice, big rock. There's no shortage of rocks on the Caja.

"What are you going to do, try to brain the cows?" I asked.

"Those are steers," Rusty said.

"Whatever," I said. "Are you going to antagonize them by hurling rocks?

"No," said Rusty. "I'm just going to try to drive the bigger one off. If he goes, the smaller one will probably follow." He hurled the rock and it bounced off the steer. The steer didn't budge.

"Nice shot," I said, eying the tree.

Rusty hurled another rock and the two bovines continued to watch us as they finally moseyed along, placid as could be. Grant came back when the cows were at a safe distance. He said, "I think we're lost."

Rusty said, "I think you're right."

Rusty, of course, was very embarrassed because he was raised in Santa Fe and swore that he knew the Caja like the back of his hand. Grant was kicking himself because he's an orienteering freak and NEVER gets lost. Diane was still trying to identify familiar-looking piles of turd – and pottery shards. And, I was quietly panicking because it was getting dark and cold and we didn't know where the hell we were.

I pulled Grant aside and said, "You know all those droppings Diane was pointing out earlier?"

"Yeah," he said.

"Well, tonight, all the animals that left those droppings are going to come out to hunt and WE are going to be those droppings tomorrow."

"Holy shit," said Grant.

"Well, I'm not religious – but, yeah."

"Not to mention, I'm not going to make it to Atlanta, which is where I'm moving back to if I ever make it out of here alive. To tell you the truth, I think we're in a life-threatening situation, and I'm not happy about it."

"You actually think we're in a life-threatening situation?"

"Well, let's see – we're out in the middle of the desert in February with night approaching. We're out of water, we have no food, our cell phones don't work, we don't know where we are and we're in a place with a whole shit-load of wild animal droppings. Plus, I'm really getting pissed off because we've actually walked around twenty miles today instead of eight – or even fifteen – and my feet are starting to hurt. You do the math."

We trudged along. Rusty suggested that we split up, but I nixed that idea completely. We each took a walkie-talkie – in case we accidentally got separated – and walked in circles until a mountain range suddenly looked familiar. By this time, the sun had set and it was getting quite nippy out.

Rusty gave Diane a handgun and said, "I think we're within a couple of miles of the truck. Why don't you girls sit behind a tree with Hercules and wait for us."

I asked, "What's the gun for?"

Rusty said, "There could be some mean cowboys out here."

Ah – that's just what was missing from the picture – mean cowboys out on the Caja in the dark. This was getting better and better.

I gave Grant a look and told him to keep in touch on the walkie-talkie. Diane bravely assured me that if worse came to worse, we could huddle together for warmth and barbecue the dog. Oh, really? Did somebody have a match or were we going to have to rub two sticks together?

"So," I said to Hercules, "I guess this isn't going to work out too well for you." Hercules panted at me with a big smile on his face – like he was thinking that maybe he would eat ME.

Time crawled – and we still hadn't heard from the boys. After about a half-hour had passed, I finally buzzed Grant on the walkie-talkie and, much to my delight, he actually answered. He sounded a bit glum.

"Hi, sweetie," I said with hysterical cheer. "Did you find the truck?"

After a thirty-second lapse, Grant said, "Yeah." After another thirty-second lapse, I said, "Truck doesn't work, does it?"

"No."

And, there you go. Or not. I mean, Jesus H. I shut my squawky walkie-talkie off and prepared to eat dog.

Diane, of course, heard the entire conversation – not that it was very long.

"What I wouldn't give for a mean cowboy right now," I said.

Suddenly, we heard the sound of a rasping motor.

"That's the truck," we said in unison.

We were thrilled, of course – but probably no more so than Hercules.

As the truck came bouncing down the road with the rear door open, Rusty yelled, "Jump in." I think he was afraid the motor would stall if he stopped. So, Diane and I and the dog all hurled ourselves across the back seat and off we sped.

"You're not going to believe this, Rusty," I said after I got out from underneath Diane and Hercules, "but, minutes after you guys walked off, a massive herd of wild horses ran within twenty feet of us. There must've been five hundred of them. What a shame that you missed them."

I don't think I ever told Rusty I was just screwing with him. And, since Diane had to suck down an entire container of ginger mints on the way home, I don't think she ever told him either.

And, yes, I did make it to Atlanta the next day. And, yes, we have taken many other hikes with our dear friends, Rusty and Diane and their now-departed dog, Hercules, who died of natural causes.

ROCKY MOUNTAIN HIGH

My mother is spending a few months in Boulder, Colorado this summer, where it is always 1969. It brings back the memory of sitting at the kitchen table with my mother and brother on Long Island that very year, getting stoned before my father got home from work. It was my mother's one and only adventure with "marahoochee." She still can't say marijuana. But, it wasn't marijuana that was in my brother's hash pipe, so what does it matter?

MAMA DOES MARAHOOCHEE

JULY 2012

My big brother was always a major pothead. Back in the late sixties, he would come home from Penn State with his little pipe and tin foil and spend hours sucking down turd-like pellets of black hash. At sixteen, I had smoked a little weed myself, but this opiated shit he was bringing home really knocked the garden-variety stuff out of the park.

My parents knew he was smoking something in his room but it was a sign of the times that they didn't attempt to stop him. What else did he have to do when he was home from school?

I was a relative newcomer to mind-altering drugs and didn't care for them much – they made me paranoid. Like, if my boyfriend wanted to get me stoned with the intention of relieving me of my virginity, he would've been better off giving me a cup of black coffee. You live and learn.

At any rate, one night, when my father announced he would be coming home late, my mother barged into my brother's room and said, "Okay, bring out the marahoochee – I want to see what all the noise is about."

My brother was more than happy to oblige her. He didn't take into account that our mother was a chain smoker and, therefore, was the only one in the family who actually knew how to inhale. And, inhale she did –

she inhaled herself straight to another planet.

We gathered around the gray Formica table in the narrow kitchen and watched my brother carefully install a glob of hash into the foiled bowl of his pipe like he was performing brain surgery. He instructed my mother to hold the pipe in her mouth and inhale while he ignited the hash with his Bic. The air filled with the sweet smell of delirium, and it didn't take very long. This was some strong shit.

My mother started to condemn herself immediately. With the first exhale, out came a spate of words. "Boy, am I stupid," she said. "Man, am I going to get sick. I must be out of my mind." She inhaled again and the little black substance glowed malevolently. I kissed the pipe myself, and the corners of the room curled up.

My mother was suddenly clinging to my shoulders like a child, saying, "I think I'm going to die." Well, we couldn't have that. How would we explain that to my father, who was probably on his way home on the Long Island Railroad at that moment?

"I'm going to call 911," I announced. I even picked up the receiver.

My brother, who was rolling around on the kitchen floor, said, "No! Don't! You're bringing down my whole head."

"I'll bring down your head, all right," I said. "Mom is sick as a dog and you're worrying about losing your high?" I was the ultimate buzz kill that night.

My mother, in the meantime, was on my brother's side. "Don't call anyone," she said. "We'll all get busted."

Now, *that* wouldn't be pretty.

I pulled our mother onto the back steps to give her some air and I think she may have gotten even more polluted. My brother and I finally propped her up on the floor in the living room with her head between two stereo speakers. We may have put on Joe Cocker, or someone equally afflicted. My brother suggested that she "feel the vibes," which sounded outdated even forty years ago. "Listen to the music and don't drop dead" would've been a better choice of words but he was too shitfaced to come up with something practical. I was still watching walls curling myself, so what good was I?

We peeled our mother off the floor and got the smoke out of the house before our father got home. As we yanked her up, she said, "I don't want to ever hear the word marahoochee again." Since we had never heard the word marahoochee before, we were able to assure her it would not become a part of our vocabulary.

Our father came in exhausted, as usual. He either didn't notice that his whole family was stoned off its ass or he was too tired to care. He was hungry, but my mother wasn't a good cook under the best of circumstances. She could've fried up a Michelin tire for him and he would've eaten it with a matzo. So, my brother managed to make it back to college unscathed.

However, a few days after he left, my father was driving me home from my job at the local X-rated movie theater (for films that would be rated PG now) and said, "I understand you had a little party with your mother a few nights ago."

So, the cat was out of the – ahem – bag. Dad wasn't as clueless as he looked. But, somehow, the world continued to turn on its axis. My father gave me a little smile and said, "I come home late one night and my house becomes an opium den." Then, he dropped the matter because Mom wasn't dead, she wasn't more addled than usual, my brother was back at school and I was an innocent bystander, possibly with a little residual brain damage.

Of course, my mother's dreams of becoming president were foiled (at least, back in those days). Everything has a price.

PARTS IS PARTS

Yes, I know I am borrowing from an old Wendy's commercial, but "Parts is Parts" is shorter than "How I Spent My Summer Vacation Contemplating the Ceiling While Waiting for My Various Parts to Heal." As I write this, I am happy to report that I can now do cartwheels (which is strange because I was never able to do them before) and I'm back to singing in the rain (which any turkey can tell you is a good way to drown), but walking is still somewhat of a challenge. Nevertheless, my feet are back on the ground, and, for that, I am eternally grateful.

THESE BOOTS ARE NOT MADE FOR WALKING

AUGUST 2012

From the moment we left for Colorado, I became obsessed with the potted azaleas we left behind in Santa Fe.

"I nearly watered those plants to death," I told my husband as we pulled out of the driveway at the beginning of our trip. "Surely, they'll survive five days without more watering."

"Surely," said my husband.

"The first thing I'm going to do when we get home is water those azaleas," I said.

"Sounds like a plan," he said.

I don't know why I was so concerned about a few plants. It may be that I live in a beige land, even with the world's most colorful sunsets. I have a hell of a time keeping anything alive on my rear portal (that sounds bizarre, even as I write it).

The back of my house faces east toward the Sangre de Cristo Mountains, the southernmost part of the Rockies chain. It gets good morning sun and then it falls into the shadows for the rest of the day. I've had many a plant die on me over the past several years. Indeed, I left moist, green Atlanta – and a whole yard full of beautiful, blossoming azaleas – in 2005. I left crying and bereft, just about the way I arrived in Atlanta twenty-six years before from Boston, where I left behind a few ferns and an entire ocean.

"Why are you trying to grow azaleas in Santa Fe?" asked a friend.

"Because the container said they would do well in morning light," I replied. I didn't think about the tons of water they would need to survive in the desert.

So, my husband and I returned from our five days in Colorado. I went directly to the kitchen sink to fill a plastic container with mineral-rich well water and out I went. Suddenly, I found myself airborne. I saw myself fall in slow motion. It took a long time to hit the ground, but, when I did, I knew I had broken something.

I had never broken a bone before – unless you count the time I swam into the side of a pool in Toronto and fractured my nose. But, fracturing your nose doesn't lay you up for months, whereas a broken fifth metatarsal will fuck up your life for a long time – and force you to wear unattractive, cumbersome footwear.

And, here's the kicker – the azaleas, now known as the freaking azaleas, were dead anyway.

The first doctor I went to was my regular family practitioner. He looked at my foot and said, "How the hell did you do that?"

I replied, "Freaking azaleas," which he didn't quite get. I must have still been in a state of shock.

He sent me off to get X-rays, which confirmed that my left foot was broken. I was shipped off to a podiatrist – the first of three.

The first guy came in with a big smile on his face and told me I had a fracture with a name.

I said, "What? – like Irving?"

He said, "No – like Jones."

He then told me that it's not good when a fracture is named after somebody. He told me that this fracture would require surgery because the place I broke my foot didn't have a blood supply. Somebody would need to jam a big screw in my foot to encourage it to heal. He then told me to take nine Advil a day and slapped a boot on my foot that made me walk like Frankenstein. I sat in the parking lot of a CVS crying while my husband bought a bottle containing ten thousand Advil. I was convinced the pills would destroy my liver, but I was considering washing them down with an arsenic cocktail anyway. Frankly, I was having trouble relating to being hobbled and overmedicated for an indeterminate period of time. And, I'm terrified of surgery.

Two days later, I met with the second podiatrist who told me I did not have a Jones fracture. I had an avulsion fracture, which would eventually heal on its own – maybe. He told me to stay off my foot and come back to see him in a month. My husband figured I would kill myself – or him – with crutches – so he got me a contraption called a knee rollator. Speak of killing yourself. The rollator had "Ben-Hur"-like Roman chariot wheels, featuring great, big protruding rear axles that nearly broke my right ankle. It also gave me a spectacular case of bursitis in my left hip. I took to wearing a snow boot on my good foot for protection – in June, when it was over ninety degrees every day.

In the meantime, I was convinced that the Frankenstein boot – detailed in metal and Velcro – was attracting lightning. I kept getting bolts of pain traveling up my left leg. The doctor told me this was nothing unusual – that nerve pain was part of the healing process. Nevertheless, between the boot and the rollator, I was experiencing torture on wheels.

I spent the better part of six weeks flat on my back in my front room. If you need to choose a room to recuperate in, my front room is the place to do it. It has magnificent views of the Jemez Mountains to the west and my front portal, which contains a lovely burbling fountain. It has very nice light, a comfortable couch and a paddle fan. I was okay in there until I got deathly ill with some kind of strange sickness that robbed me of both my voice and my sanity. For several days, I sounded like Ned Beatty squealing in "Deliverance."

In my fevered mind, I surmised this was the universe telling me to "Sit down and shut up."

I finally bit the bullet and put myself on a round of antibiotics when I realized, after two weeks, that I wasn't getting better. I stopped squealing after the third week and, much to some people's chagrin, I began talking incessantly instead. I was still considering a nice cyanide Mai Tai or maybe a trip to Lourdes because the whole affair had left me depressed, exhausted and muddle-headed, which isn't a good look for me.

When I returned to the second podiatrist, he told me my foot looked beautiful. I thought the coral nail polish was a nice touch. Unfortunately, my foot was still broken and he hadn't ruled out surgery. I told him I hadn't ruled out suicide. He smiled like he knew I was just joshing. I smiled because he didn't know about the rat poison I was carrying in my handbag. (*Now*, I'm joshing. Not only did I not have rat poison in my purse; I didn't have cyanide in my fridge. You should know that threatening to kill myself is how I occasionally make it through an annoying day. Nobody wants to live more than I do. Please forgive me for mentioning suicide eighty-seven times in this story.)

Getting back to the second podiatrist, he told me he wanted me in the boot for another four weeks but he wanted to see me in three. (For what?

To taunt me about the possibility of surgery some more?) He told me I could lose the rollator and that as long as I took off my boot while I was in my car I could drive.

Ah, freedom! Perhaps I would allow myself to live another day. Turns out, he wasn't going to be around in three weeks and I didn't want to see the first joker. So, I scheduled myself to see a third podiatrist.

I spent the next three weeks taking my boot on and off a hundred times a day. Occasionally, I would forget to take the boot off when I got behind the wheel of the car and would damn near get killed trying to take it off in the middle of the highway going seventy-five miles an hour lest I get stopped by a cop and arrested for driving while impersonating Frankenstein. Anyway, the three weeks passed and I got to see podiatrist number three.

The third podiatrist was certainly my favorite because he was the one who told me I was ninety-five percent healed and that I didn't need to come back. He asked me how I was feeling. I said, "I plan to dance out of here."

"You can dance out of here but only if you know the steps because I can't teach you any," he said.

Great! I had a podiatrist with a sense of humor and good news (except for the part about keeping the boot handy because my foot was likely to hurt and throw me off balance and make me walk like Grandpappy Amos in "The Real McCoys" for quite a while to come.)

The first thing I did was kick off my boots, which are not made for walking (only healing, which I've mostly done) and put on a pair of old ballet-style shoes (which are also not made for walking, but for dancing.) I went off to my gym, which I had not worked out in for two months, and discovered that I had lost neither strength nor flexibility. I was still muddle-headed, strangely – that's what prolonged imbalance can do to you – but at least l felt like life was back on track again.

That's when I noticed that lots of the people around me were in boots! Big, high black boots; heavy, honking metal boots; boots with plastic inserts – all kinds of goofy boots, along with canes and walkers and crutches and rollators. I felt like I was in a Fellini movie. And, I felt a new sense of kinship with all these people who yanked themselves off their couches, affixed their handicapped placards to their rearview mirrors and used whatever healthy parts were available to them while their damaged parts healed.

And, isn't that what it's all about?

HORSING AROUND IN NORTH GEORGIA

You already know this is going to be a silly story involving foursomes and horses and sexual innuendos. I'm going to preface it with a short love story. My husband and I were taking a ride in the North Georgia Mountains one day when I saw a spectacular white horse in a field. The horse saw me, too, and came running. In fact, we both ran toward each other with our manes flying, like we were in a Clairol commercial. When we were practically nose-to-nose, I reached for him and he reached for me, and the next thing I knew I was flying across the road to the sound of distant neighing. Neither of us saw the electrified fence that came between us. Relationships are complicated.

FUN WITH DICK AND DICK

OCTOBER 2012

I don't know what the deal is, but about twenty years ago, my husband and I must have had some kind of allure. Other couples were approaching us for nights of swinging abandon. I mean, really – it was flattering and ridiculous at the same time. And, there was always a guy named "Dick" involved. How perfect is that?

First, one of my husband's friends asked if we would like to join him and his wife for a weekend at a place in the North Georgia Mountains called The End of the Road. We would have separate cabins and enjoy simple pleasures like horseback riding – if you find that pleasurable.

I ended up with a nice enough horse, named Apple Dumpling or Sugar Cube. She was a sweet old nag with a beard. My husband, on the other hand, had a huge stallion named Black Death, or something, and the horse kept breathing on me like he wanted to bite my leg off. That's how close the horses were on the trail. But, I digress – I was talking about a horse of a different color.

We decided to take Dick up on his invitation. We drove up on a

25

Friday. Our cabin was rustic with a big hot tub sunk into the dark, woodsy living room.

Outside of horseback riding and soaking, there wasn't a whole lot to do at The End of the Road. So, we took Dick and his wife, who looked like Little Miss Muffet, to Helen, a theme-park town that's all dressed up like Bavaria. It was October and Oktoberfest was in full swing. The town was jammed with people swigging Lowenbrau out of big paper cups and there was polka music in the air.

We all had several brewskies before heading back to The End of the Road. Somehow, we survived the ride on dark and winding mountain roads to accept a nightcap at Dick and Miss Muffet's cabin.

The nightcap for Dick turned out to be a big joint. The rest of us just sat around making small talk over the hot tub that dominated the room. Dick's wife was seated on the floor in front of me and I found it a little strange when she wrapped her arms around my legs and placed her head in my lap. Hmmm. This was a blond-haired mother of three young children. Maybe she was just tired and ready for sleepy time. That's what I thought right up until the moment she looked up at me with round saucer eyes and asked, "Can we all get naked now?" She gave my thighs a little squeeze when she asked.

I looked at my husband, my husband looked at me, we both looked at Dick, nobody looked at the wife and my husband made a definitive declaration. "That wouldn't be convenient," he said.

I gently flipped Miss Muffet onto her tuffet and we fled back to our cabin. We had to get up early to hit the road anyway.

"What the hell was that?" I asked my husband.

"I can't be sure, but I think we were just propositioned," he said.

"Seriously? Who are we, Mr. and Mrs. Buck Naked?"

"Apparently, they thought so."

Interesting, but really not convenient. I guess the idea was to get a little drunk and have a sexual adventure with another couple in a hot tub. Frankly, I would've preferred to have a go at my husband's horse. Black Death was really intense.

When we met to say goodbye the next morning, Dick and his wife acted as if nothing had happened – and, of course, nothing had. I'm glad they were not offended because they were really a delightful couple.

Skip forward a week – another couple, another Dick – this one with a Brazilian wife. We had met them at a delicatessen.

Dick looked like a thin version of my husband – a tall, Nordic type from someplace like Bismarck, North Dakota. The wife was more exotic – dark skinned and, well, Brazilian – and, around twenty-five. Dick was intrigued from the get-go. He started to call me right after we had indulged in salami together.

Eventually, we decided to have dinner out, the four of us. They invited us to their house first, for a glass of wine. Everything was progressing normally until the wife brought out Madonna's self-aggrandizing *SEX* book and started flipping through the shots.

"I think that Madonna is the most beautiful woman in the world," said Dick, without looking at the book. He looked from me to his wife and remarked, "Madonna puts the two of you to shame."

My husband said, "You're entitled to your opinion, but I find our wives far more beautiful than Madonna."

That was just the opening they needed and, again, it was the wife who initiated the action. She closed the book and gave me a leering look. "Your husband thinks we're hotter than Madonna. Maybe we should stay in instead of going out," she cooed.

Dick stood there, coolly sipping his wine, waiting for the verdict.

I looked at my husband, my husband looked at me, we both looked at Dick, nobody looked at the wife and, this time, *I* said, "That wouldn't be convenient."

That, and I didn't want salami for dinner.

I don't recall if we made it out or not, but we did suggest they spend a weekend up at The End of the Road with a couple we knew. We suspected that somewhere between the horses and the hot tubs, they would all find what they were looking for.

CELERY, ANYONE?

I love the holiday season – all the gatherings with family and friends and the festivities over meals. I have vivid memories of eating wild game off of Santa Claus plates, of getting stoned on Manishewitz at Seders and of waiting for hours for briskets to cook at high altitude. My most memorable holiday, though, took place a few years ago – the first Thanksgiving I ever hosted. It was an event in which every guest had dietary restrictions and the trick was to fix a traditional meal that wouldn't land anyone in the emergency room. I am thankful to say, "We did it!"

INDIANS FOR THANKSGIVING

NOVEMBER 2012

It all starts when I hear from Indian friends from Cleveland that my husband and I haven't seen in five years – and when I say Indian, I mean the elephant kind, not the buffalo kind. Ravi and Preeta want to come visit and the day they select is November twenty-second. I look it up on the calendar and say, "But that's Thanksgiving."

They say, "We don't care. We don't celebrate."

"Well, we do," I say, "but we don't have any plans for this year, so you are more than welcome to come."

When my friend, Diane, learns that we're having Indians for Thanksgiving, she asks me what I'm planning to serve.

"I don't know. Some kind of vindaloo, I imagine."

I ask Diane if she and her husband, Rusty, would like to join us.

"Of course," she says, "but not for vindaloo. It's Thanksgiving."

"But they don't celebrate Thanksgiving," I say. "Plus, she doesn't eat poultry and he's gluten-intolerant. They may be vegetarians altogether."

"Well, I have a nut allergy and Rusty doesn't eat sweets, but it's Thanksgiving and we're coming for dinner," says Diane. "While we're at it,

28

let's invite Maxine and Harold."

"I love Maxine and Harold," I say, "but, Harold is diabetic and he can't eat sugar and Maxine bakes pies with artificial sweetener that keeps us up all night."

Actually, Maxine bakes fabulous pies. I'm just worried she'll find out I don't know my ass from my giblets about preparing a traditional Thanksgiving meal. That, and I'm afraid Harold will end up face down in his yams because he's also narcoleptic.

"No buts," says Diane. "We're all coming to your house for Thanksgiving and it won't be for vindaloo."

"I have to admit something to you," I say. "I've never prepared a Thanksgiving dinner in my life. I'm concerned about killing everyone in the house with the turkey – even the vegetarians who may eat it accidentally. What if I don't cook it right?"

"Any idiot can cook a turkey," says Diane. "Just use a meat thermometer and everything will be fine."

"Okay," I say, throwing up my hands. At least I won't kill Preeta with the turkey, because, for her, I will have to prepare fish. Maybe I'll kill Ravi with the turkey. I think I saw him eat chicken once.

Then, Diane tells me that her husband, Rusty, a former bull rider with the rodeo, is going to make the gravy and that I should save my giblets for him.

"What if the turkey doesn't have any giblets?" I ask.

"There'll be giblets, don't worry," Diane says. "Just cook them along with the bird and he'll do the rest when we get there. We'll bring mashed potatoes and a green bean casserole, too."

I call Preeta back and tell her we're going to have a traditional Thanksgiving meal when they arrive on Thanksgiving Day.

"That sounds great," she says. "I will bring a gluten-free pie and a box of cornflakes for Ravi's breakfast."

"You're going to bring a box of cornflakes on the plane? Seriously? I'll buy you a box of cornflakes."

"No", she says, "I absolutely insist. "I will bring a gluten-free pie and a box of cornflakes."

"You will be my guest," I say. "I will supply the cornflakes. Now, I must insist. There will be cornflakes awaiting Ravi in my kitchen."

"No!" Preeta says. "You must let me bring the cornflakes."

"Fine," I say. What else am I going to say? I mentally cross cornflakes off my shopping list.

I call Maxine and she and Harold agree to join us on Thanksgiving Day and they are excited to meet our guests from Cleveland. Maxine, who is a gourmet cook, wants to know what she can bring. In reality, she wants to bring the entire meal. Had I requested it, I'll bet she would've made a mean vindaloo – but I promised Preeta a traditional Thanksgiving meal.

"Well," I say, "I'm going to make the turkey and cranberry relish and yams and pecan pie and crescent rolls. Rusty's making the gravy and Diane's making the mashed potatoes and green beans. And, Preeta's bringing a gluten-free pie and a box of cornflakes."

"What are the cornflakes for?" Maxine inquires.

"Ravi is gluten-intolerant."

"Oh," says Maxine.

"How about a salad and a pumpkin pie?" I suggest.

Everybody has an assignment. Mine is trying to figure out how to cook before a bunch of people show up – one who can't eat poultry, one who can't eat nuts, one who can't eat sugar, many who can't eat sugar substitute, one who is gluten-intolerant, one who wants fish, one who can't drink alcohol (my tee-totaling husband) and two who aren't observant and don't give a damn about Thanksgiving.

I go out and buy a meat thermometer and a bag to cook – and possibly bury – the turkey in. Thanksgiving is still a couple of weeks off. I begin to collect recipes. And, I start drinking early – which is okay with my husband, even though he can't personally drink alcohol.

Maxine calls several times to ascertain that she's supposed to make pumpkin pie instead of pecan. I have visions of having mass quantities of pecan pie and nothing else, which will deprive Diane of a dessert – unless Ravi is willing to share his gluten-free pie, which I suspect may have nuts in it.

The day arrives and there's pandemonium in my kitchen. I've prepared the cranberries and yams and pecan pies in advance. The turkey is roasting away in its bag. Rusty is decked out in a frilly apron, looking like Buffalo Bob in a pinafore. He's concerned about the paucity of my giblets.

"Why are there so few giblets?" he asks.

"What can I tell you?" I respond. "I did a complete cavity search and that's all I was able to find."

What the hell, there was something that looked like a scrawny neck and a few shriveled innards to mix in with the drippings. To make up for the giblet deficiency, Rusty decides to throw in three pounds of flour.

That's when Maxine and Harold show up. Maxine has the requested salad and pumpkin pie in tow but, in addition, she has also brought rolls. I quietly slip two cans of crescents back into the fridge.

"These came out terrible," Maxine announces. "They're going to taste just like golf balls."

Nevertheless, the golf balls are all duded up in gingham and nestled in a basket, so I know they're going to be on the table. They are certainly pretty enough to eat – off a tee.

As Maxine progresses into my kitchen, she notices Rusty flailing away at the gravy and decides it needs some milk. I playfully brandish a fork at her and snarl, "Don't mess with Rusty's gravy. I don't care if it tastes like motor oil." It was Rusty's gravy, after all.

By this time, Ravi and Preeta have fallen in from Cleveland, minus the gluten-free pie.

"What happened to the pie?" I inquire.

"Oh, it collapsed so I didn't bring it," says Preeta.

"Well, then, Ravi will have to have pie filling," I say. "He'll have a choice of pecan goo or pumpkin goo, whichever he prefers."

We lay out the dinner and everything is perfect. Nobody dies from the turkey. All the fixings are delicious – even Rusty's floury, giblet-deficient gravy. Nobody ends up spending the night in the toilet. Before everyone leaves, Maxine exclaims, "This was the best Thanksgiving ever! We're coming again next year!" I am deeply thankful to have such wonderful friends.

The next morning, when our guests come into the kitchen for breakfast, Preeta asks, "Is there anything for Ravi to eat?"

"Where are your cornflakes?" I ask.

"I didn't bring them."

...Huh?

...Next year, we'll celebrate Thanksgiving in Poona..

POULTRY IN MOTION

The expression, "When you gotta go, you gotta go," never meant more than when my husband and I were trying to make it home to Santa Fe from Boulder in gale force winds, getting pelted with everything from tumbleweed to flying turkeys ahead of a snowstorm and searching for a pot to pee in or a tree to hide behind in New Mexico without getting blown away or arrested. The whole trip was more fun than squirting whipped cream on pecan pie. Imagine that.

WHEN YOU GOTTA GO

DECEMBER 2012

After a delightful Thanksgiving with family in Boulder, my husband and I said our good-byes, sucked up our gut and got in the car for our return trip to Santa Fe ahead of what was threatening to be a big snowstorm. At least the weatherman was threatening – the guy was a maniacal prophet of doom. On the morning of our departure, the sky was blue and the sun was blazing, but we were assured that a tidal wave of icy destruction was blowing in from the west – so we were going to haul ass out of there.

The fun started about a mile from my brother's house, when my husband decided to stop at a coffee shop and get his dose of caffeine for the ride ahead. In his enthusiasm, he failed to notice that he'd parked in a bus stop and, since we had already gotten a ticket for going a mile over the speed limit in Boulder on a previous trip, I pointed out that we might get a jail sentence for parking in a bus stop for three minutes. My husband agreed and backed up so he could find another spot and I heard a bang because he'd backed up without looking.

"Holy shit, sweetie," I said, "Did you hit a curb?"

"No," he said. "I hit a man."

"What????"

"This is just what I need," he said, as he exited our vehicle. My husband had already jacked our insurance premiums up to about a million dollars a year for backing and fronting and siding up into various inanimate objects. This time, I was afraid he had actually run someone over.

Turns out, he had backed into someone's hundred-thousand-dollar Jaguar, with the guy sitting in the car. Hey, if you have to crash into something, you might as well aim for a ridiculously expensive vintage vehicle. By the time I poked my head out to see what was going on, the two guys were surveying their bumpers for damage. Fortunately, both cars seemed to be okay. I asked the guy if he was all right – nice touch – and I was truly grateful that he said, "Yes." After the guy gave us permission to leave, my husband got back in the car and said, "I'm not having coffee here. We're leaving right now." And, we sped the hell away, without hitting anything, thank God.

Of course, the next part of the trip became about finding a coffee shop while the ominous weather system continued its menacing crawl toward us, as the sun continued to blast. We passed many places and somehow managed to just miss the entrance to all of them.

"I think I forgot my nightgown," I announced as we approached Superior. "Good," said my husband because that gave him the opportunity to pull off the road to look for a coffee shop that was bound to be around there somewhere that would offer me the chance to open our bag and look for my lingerie. The nightie was there, my husband got his coffee and we finally took off with the dreaded storm about a half hour closer.

Things got interesting as we approached Colorado Springs. We started taking turns white-knuckling it down the highway in a high-wind advisory that only intensified as we progressed along. Fortunately, there were only about twelve other cars on the road, and all the drivers had their hands in the ten and two position and their bodies thrust forward, like conscientious driver's ed. students on their first ride out.

As the car swayed to and fro, we got pelted in the windshield with tumbleweed and gravel. And, near the New Mexico border, we nearly got taken out by a flying turkey.

"What the hell was that?" I inquired.

"That was a wild turkey," said my husband.

"What is it, an escapee? And, since when do turkeys fly?"

I scanned the sky for flying bowls of yams and cranberry sauce.

"Oh, turkeys fly," my husband said calmly. "They just don't fly very far."

"No, just into our windshield, that's all."

I get sarcastic sometimes.

"This one might be injured," said my husband. "I don't know why else it would be flying across the road."

"How about to get to the other side?" I suggested. Then I got concerned that determined hunters with big wild turkey guns might have panicked the turkey into flying across the road. I didn't want the next thing flying through the windshield to turn us into road kill. The turkey was fine. We just needed to move down the highway.

In southern Colorado, we stopped at a rest stop to unclench our knuckles. I was going to try to get to the bathroom from the car but was afraid I would blow away in the high winds. That's when I noticed there wasn't a woman in the parking lot that weighed less than three hundred pounds.

"I'm going to make a run for it," I told my husband. "If I start to fly away, I'm going to hold onto one of those sturdy ladies."

I weaved my way through the parking lot in the shelter of the big women like I was dodging bullets on a battlefield and made it back to the car the same way. I suggested that my husband do the same because, after his cup of coffee, he was guzzling a five-hundred-ounce can of iced tea and I figured he would have to get rid of it pretty soon. Unfortunately, he didn't have to go at that moment.

Then we stopped at a Cracker Barrel in Pueblo for lunch. I was attracted to a quilt in the gift shop, so the lunch ended up costing us over a hundred dollars. My husband bought four Andes Candies, which he forgot about – so he ended up with chocolate pockets – and he still wasn't in the mood to take a leak. The man has a bladder like a camel – until it's full and then he enters a state of amazing urgency.

So, we blew our way into New Mexico. We stopped for gas in Las Vegas – driving against the wind reduced our gas efficiency to about two miles to the gallon. My husband's bladder suddenly went into overdrive. He ran knock-kneed to the gas station restroom and discovered fifteen men waiting on line. He didn't want to wait. I didn't want to wait either because it looked like the highly-advertised snowstorm was getting ready to hit and it was getting dark, too. I suggested that he try the Burger King next door, but the bathroom was padlocked there altogether, so we just took off, anticipating rest stops along the way.

Unfortunately, in the state of New Mexico, rest stops, more often than not, do not have facilities. I don't know what the hell you're supposed to do at a rest stop without facilities, aside from stay in your car and play with yourself because, even if you were considering relieving yourself behind a bush, there are big signs everywhere that warn "Disposal of Human Waste is Strictly Prohibited" – and you gotta know that there is probably some idiot from the police department assigned to the rest stop to monitor the situation – because, in the Land of Enchantment, the police are more interested in catching a middle-aged Anglo relieving himself in a No-Peeing Zone than catching gang bangers raping and pillaging old ladies in their living rooms.

I told my husband he could either pee on the sign – which would probably come with a stiff jail sentence – or drive cross-legged for a while. He decided to do the latter because it's hard to find a bush in The Land of Enchantment. It's a damned desert, for Christ's sake.

We continued to get buffeted for the next hour or so and continued to pass rest stops with no facilities, whole towns without bathrooms and whole forests without bushes. And, then, before we knew it, we were home.

And, the snowstorm never came.

HELLO MUDDAH, HELLO FADDAH...

When Allan Sherman wrote his hilarious parody about the fictional Camp Granada in 1963, I had no personal experience with sleep-away camp. So, when I became a counselor at Camp Ma-Ho-Ge in 1970, I was wondering if I would actually encounter alligators in the lake. What did I know? It was my first time away from home. And, no, there were no alligators – only crayfish.

Today, it's great to see generations of Ma-Ho-Geans reconnecting on Facebook (and in person) and sharing precious memories. Here are mine.

THE LAST OF THE MA-HO-GEANS

JANUARY 2013

After never having gone to a sleep-away camp myself, I became a counselor at Camp Ma-Ho-Ge in the summer of 1970. My cousin, Mitchell, turned me on to it. I was a seventeen-year-old high school student and this was my first time away from home; at least, it was my first summer of doing something other than stay in a bungalow colony or take a road trip with my family. It certainly was the first time I shared living quarters and a bathroom with a dozen or more strangers and slept in a bunk bed. I loved it!

One summer, I had girls who were almost as old as I was. I remember the faces of many of my campers. And, I'm still in touch with my bunkmate, Amy. We also went to high school together.

There are a few memories that stand out more than others. Some are pretty bizarre. For example, I remember, in my first year, standing clueless in a bathroom stall while my senior counselor shouted instructions on how to insert a tampon. I'm sure the applicator came out eventually.

I remember my one and only camping experience. It was a rainy night and I led a bunk full of little girls into the woods for a night in the great outdoors. I finally got them settled down and ready for a bedtime story. Unfortunately, that story was told by a lifeguard who had come along for the hike and it was all about the "Cropsey Monster" – aka the boogeyman – who kidnapped (and, according to the lifeguard, fed on) children. That was an unfortunate choice. What was even more unfortunate was that I had a sleeping bag with a broken zipper and an unwanted visitor – a skunk who tried to snuggle in to get dry. So, after the little girls and I stopped screaming, we all gathered our belongings and took a soggy walk back to the bunk.

Sadly, I attracted skunks all summer. They seemed to show up late at night when I was on babysitting duty, just sitting there with my salami sandwich minding my own business. Getting sprayed by a skunk on the way to a tryst with the lifeguard in the middle of the night was also a drag. It's not like we had vats of tomato sauce to dump over our heads to get rid of the smell.

I remember another adventure in which I had a rowboat full of little girls out on the lake. We were going fishing. What did I know about fishing? Nothing. We were using Cheerios for bait and all we caught were our socks. We also managed to catch a crayfish. Once that sucker was in the boat, all the little girls jumped overboard and I had to save them because they really didn't know how to swim yet. Good thing I was trained as a lifeguard, too.

Nineteen-seventy was the year after Woodstock, right there in good old Bethel. One night, another counselor and I decided to go to Max Yasgur's Farm and check out the scene. All traces of the festival were gone, but we decided to reenact peace and love on a blanket taken from his bunk. Suddenly, a light was shining in our eyes. A New York State trooper had discovered us canoodling in the grass. We said we were counselors at a nearby camp and he told us he would escort us home. After I got into the car, my buddy said, "Don't panic but I have a huge stash of drugs in the glove compartment."

Jesus! Don't panic? Of course, I was going to panic – but the cop never checked. We were lucky. We could've landed in Sing Sing.

I had another boyfriend at Ma-Ho-Ge. His name was Hy and he was also a counselor. During color war, he was a general with the Grey Astronauts, but he called himself Chief Hy Howaya. I loved that the teams were blue and grey – just like we were fighting the Civil War. My mother-in-law, who was a Daughter of the Confederacy, would've loved that.

Two life-altering events occurred during my tenure at Ma-Ho-Ge. One occurred in my first summer and one occurred in my second.

In the first, I came back to my bunk to find a newspaper article on my bed. The article was about a friend from high school who was spending the summer in Peru as a foreign exchange student. Her plane had crashed into a mountain in the Andes and she had perished there. This was a girl I was close to; someone who I had gone through confirmation class with at Temple Emanuel in New Hyde Park. I was too young to lose a friend. I ran out of the bunk and jumped right into the lake. I think about Jerilyn to this day.

The other occurred in the summer before I started college at Brandeis. I went out for pizza with a group of counselors. I ordered a Coke with my meal. Shortly after I had a sip, I noticed that I was seeing everything from the perspective of the chair. That, in itself, was strange and disorienting. When I tried to walk, the floor was coming up toward my face and I was walking down toward the floor. I was trying to make it to a phone booth to call my parents but my voice sounded way too low. My drink had been laced.

I made it back to camp with the other counselors but instead of going back to the bunk, I wandered into the pitch-black woods. A young blond man followed me. I suspect he's the guy who laced my drink. He's also the guy who made sure I got back to my bunk. And, when I started Brandeis that fall, his face was the first I saw in the bookstore, but we didn't acknowledge each other. Maybe he was the Cropsey Monster. I certainly don't recall him being a counselor at Ma-Ho-Ge.

At any rate, in the same week, I met a woman in my dorm named Leslie and we became close friends. Turns out, her uncle was Max Yasgur!

You gotta love the smallness of our world.

So, that is the extent of my sleep-away camp experience. Camp Ma-Ho-Ge was my one and only. And, I'm happy to still be a part of its enduring community. We are the last of the Ma-Ho-Geans.

.

THE GIRL OF SUMMER

When I was a child growing up in the Bronx and Queens and Long Island, I spent summer vacations in the Catskill Mountains, usually in bungalow colonies, where fathers only came up on weekends. I spent the later years of my childhood working in the Borscht Belt, first as a camp counselor at Camp Ma-Ho-Ge and then as a cocktail waitress at Grossinger's. What could have better prepared me for life in the larger world than that?

WET AND WILD
MY LIFE AS A BORSCHT BELT COCKTAIL WAITRESS

FEBRUARY 2013

In the summer of my nineteenth year, I went to work as a cocktail waitress at Grossinger's in Liberty, New York, in the heart of the Catskill Mountains. This was in 1972, toward the end of the Borscht Belt's heyday. It was the first of two summers I spent there while I was a student at Brandeis University. Speak of getting an education!

I must say that most of the people I worked with during my tenure at Grossinger's were like myself – college kids trying to contribute to their educations. We came for a season or a Christmas break with no intention of having a career in the hospitality industry. But there were a substantial number of shady characters that were hired for a song to work as long as they wanted to – or until they killed somebody.

Because cocktail waitresses typically worked until four a.m., or until the last booze hound left the bar, we were allowed to stay in a cabin that was close to the main hotel. Most workers at Grossingers stayed together in a big fire trap out in left field. But it didn't seem like a good idea to have a group of teenaged cocktail waitresses gallivanting around in hot pants and stilettos in the middle of the night wandering toward the building where the day workers stayed. I am grateful that we were given that extra layer of protection.

The cabin had five twin beds and one small bathroom. The beds were within a few inches of each other – so when each of the cocktail waitresses had an overnight guest, it became hard to sleep.

Initially, I was sharing the cabin with three virgins, straight out of parochial schools from places like Dallas and Cape Cod and Albany. And then, there was one fully-grown woman who had a bed in the cabin but left in the middle of the night to join her boyfriend, Rocco, God knows where, and usually with our tips. We never said anything because she was twice our age and wore a wig and had a boyfriend named Rocco – what teenaged girl wouldn't have been intimidated?

By the time we were two weeks into the summer, all of the virgins had been deflowered by golf pros and pool boys. I wasn't a virgin going in – lucky me – but I was far more knowledgeable going out than coming in.

I ended up dating a guy from Canarsie whose face should have been posted at every planned parenthood clinic in the country – wanted, dead or alive. The man was the knock-up king of the Borscht Belt. There was one woman he impregnated four times – and they still couldn't figure out how to prevent it. He eventually stopped having sex with her in order to have sex with me. He was a real stand-up guy that way – and in every way, apparently. In fact, he was so fertile, I got a false positive pregnancy test from just kissing him! No, I'm not kidding.

To continue – my boyfriend – who shall remain nameless – worked in the health club and also as a stage manager in the nightclub. He was built like a Sherman tank, had a wild "Isro" (aka, a "Jewfro – not unlike mine) and occasionally talked like Donald Duck with a Brooklyn accent. His real voice sounded like something hard being ground in a garbage disposal. He quacked at my father once – and my father was not impressed (even though he was personally prone to quacking, especially on long road trips – but that's a whole other story).

Thanks to Nameless and his stage work, I got to meet and dress lots of entertainers, like Shecky Greene and Milton Berle. While I was there, Jackie Mason spent a whole summer at Grossinger's performing in "The Last of the Red-Hot Lovers." I'll bet he was, too – "know what I'm talkin' about?" He was a real ladies man.

And, while we're on the subject of entertainers, I once accidentally dropped a shot of vodka down Vic Damone's neck (but, he wasn't performing there – he was just a customer in the nightclub). He was very gracious about it.

At any rate, I enjoyed the variety that Grossinger's had to offer up and got along quite well with my cabin mates. None of them made it to the second summer, though. They were replaced by Jewish girls from places like Richmond and Tel Aviv and these Jewish girls, like myself, weren't virgins. In fact, the one from Israel was a particularly hot number with a name like Brandy Alexander (what were you expecting – Sheyna Cohen?) and she was supplementing her tips with a little mild prostitution – and by that I mean allowing the occasional customer to cop a feel for ten bucks. So, she made out better than the rest of us.

Actually, even I made out better in the second summer because Rocco's girlfriend was no longer around to filch my tips. I sure hope she didn't end up floating in the Hudson River.

I very much liked my boss, who was a Greek gentleman who treated all the waitresses with paternal respect. There was an overseer, though, who was particularly fond of taunting me in front of customers until I called him a "nasty little worm" in the service bar and that kept him away from me for the rest of the summer.

Two of the most memorable characters I met at Grossinger's worked in the staff dining room. One was Sam, the elderly manager who was an actual Grossinger family member, and one was Leo, the waiter.

One day, as I choked down my capon and kasha, Sam entered the dining room and requested attention. He cleared his throat and said, "If everyone in this room threw their package into the middle of the room, everyone would leap for their own package." That made sense to me even at the age of nineteen – and even today, for that matter.

Leo was a piece of work. He was a very heavy man with rubbery lips, a crew cut and tons of sweat. Every day, he would greet me with, "Good morning, Mrs. Rockefeller. What would you like to eat? We've got pickle juice, we've got sauerkraut juice, we've got onion juice. What is your pleasure?" When I grimaced and shook my head, he grabbed his pad and continued, "Okay, then, Mrs. Rockefeller – back to grim reality. How about some orange juice?" That was more like it.

Poor Leo. I remember the day he went running through the staff dining room with his hands flapping over his head screaming, "Nobody cares if I live or die! Nobody cares if I live or die!"

I'm glad the hysteria was short lived because I enjoyed Leo's morning spiel about the sauerkraut juice. And I got a kick out of being called "Mrs. Rockefeller."

I put in long hours in the Grossinger's nightclub and cocktail lounge, running up and down a steep flight of steps in the aforementioned stilettos, to and from the service bar, manned by a bartender named Joe. He looked like the old game show host, Bill Cullen, except with a pompadour.

Joe loved all the cocktail waitresses but he kept all his alcoholic experiments for me because I was a true lightweight. He would mix up something a poisonous shade of green and hand it to me to try. I was so naïve. Joe liked to see me tipsy because then he could get away with looking at me with hooded eyes and hissing inane innuendos like "lickety-split" or "wet and wild" while pretending to extract a pubic hair from his teeth. Nauseating, I admit. But I actually liked Joe very much. His tongue may have wiggled but he kept his hands to himself.

We never dreamed of going straight back to the cabin after a twelve-hour shift. Instead, we went down to a restaurant called the Triangle at the crack of dawn and had roast pork sandwiches. That was one thing you certainly weren't going to get at an all-Kosher resort.

It was mostly a time of innocence, but bad things occasionally happened. For example, the virgins of summer had no business in the Borscht Belt. All three of them ended up with men twice their age who took liberties. One of the girls, who had fantasies of dying in a fiery car crash, managed to land in the hospital after being raped by one of the golf pros. That wasn't the only rape that summer. There were also a few stabbing incidents. And, somebody got shot – I remember the blood stains on the hotel's flowery carpet.

But, what an ultimately great life experience it was for me.

I left the Borscht Belt in 1973 and cocktail waitressed for another couple of summers while I was at Brandeis: once at a resort in Lancaster, Pennsylvania and once at a mafia joint in Waltham, Massachusetts.

I was lured to the Amish Country by a thirty-four-year-old man who worked there. He was a professional figure skater. I had met him at the resort when I was seventeen, en route to visiting my brother at Penn State. I thought he was wonderful. He even had me dancing on ice. When he beckoned, I went.

In the Catskills, I was provided with housing. In the Amish Country, I needed to find my own digs. That ended up being in a boarding house owned by an old Mennonite lady with a broken arm and a mustache.

There was one other person living in the house – a very strange young guy who never said a word to me but who danced maniacally to "That's the Way – Uh Huh Uh Huh – I Like It" every time it came on the radio – and it came on with some great regularity back then. "Uh huh." The guy would be clicking his fingers and clapping his hands and bouncing on the bed – he was a dancing fool when that song came on. Otherwise, nothing.

If my uniform was degrading in the Catskills, it was even worse in Lancaster. It was a blood-red mini-dress with a wide black belt and matching thigh-high, high-heeled boots. Every night, I would get decked out in this attire and say "Good night" to my Mennonite landlady who, no doubt, prayed for me fervently. She liked me, though, because at least I talked to her and didn't bounce on the bed.

I didn't stick around Lancaster very long. Turns out, my friend the figure skater tried to pimp me out to a friend of his one night. I found that very unsavory, so I split and went to work as a typist for the Brandeis Women's Committee. Back then, I was such a lame typist, the other women I worked with thought I was mentally challenged. So, I left and went to work at a real bar in Waltham – the aforementioned mafia joint.

I remember the name of the joint, but I'm going to keep its name to myself because it was mob owned and operated and I don't want to expose anybody – even now. Suffice to say, I got my paychecks from a guy who asked me to call him "Godfather" – and I did.

I was twenty-two and preparing to graduate from college. The other waitresses were middle-aged townies with lots of kids and drunken husbands. They smoked Chesterfields and called everybody "Honey." I'll bet they were real thrilled about sharing their tips with me. I did make good money there and the guy in charge of entertainment used to have the band play Barry Manilow's, "Mandy" for me; except instead of "Mandy," they sang "Mindy."

It was a very sweet swan song for me because, once I graduated from college, my cocktail waitressing days were over. I was off to face the adult world of mostly fine, but occasionally grim, reality.

The Lancaster resort is still around. The mafia joint is likely gone. Grossinger's, like the rest of the Borscht Belt, is an apocalyptic ruin.

Nobody ever offered me sauerkraut juice outside of Grossinger's.

Thank you, Leo. I cared.

And, to my boyfriend from Canarsie, I loved you with all my heart. There's nothing more beautiful than a Borscht Belt romance. Thanks for the memories.

CLOSE ENCOUNTERS OF A WEIRD KIND

Since my first day of consciousness, my life has been beset with bizarre experiences. I've had visits from floating heads. I've been tormented by the antics of brownies and fairies. And my father had me convinced we were from a planet other than Earth. So, when I ran into a goat on the Appalachian Trail who appeared to emerge from a warped forest and change sizes, it was just business as usual. I'm glad my husband was with me. It's good to have a witness.

THE TRAIL GOAT

MARCH 2013

After three weeks of recovering from an outbreak of poison ivy, I was desperate to get back into the woods again. "Take me to a trail," I commanded my husband, Grant, even though it was already late in the day.

"Any trail in particular?" he asked.

"You pick," I said. "Just get me there."

I don't know why I felt so driven. Maybe it was the lingering effects of the prednisone I was allergic to.

Grant drove for about an hour and we ended up at a section of the Appalachian Trail called Neel's Gap. The sun was dipping low in the sky, and most hikers had already left. I jumped out of the car and got a head start on the trail. In fact, I was running like my hair was on fire.

About a mile in, I came to an abrupt stop. In front of me stood a tall, dark, horned creature. In fact, it looked like a huge, upright, horny man.

At first, I thought my eyes were playing tricks on me – especially because the woods to my right had an exaggerated three-dimensional look. I just stood there waiting for Grant because there was no way I could go forward with the creature on the trail and a cliff to my left. I didn't dare enter the enchanted forest on my right.

Grant saw me standing there and I pointed asking, "What the hell is that?"

Grant said, "It appears to be a really large goat. But, what would it be doing here? The nearest farm is at least four miles away."

"It's looking at me," I said. "What should we do?"

We all stood in the middle of the trail until the creature walked into the warped woods, at which time, it truly looked like a goat, and not a very large one. It was as if it were encouraging us to pass.

Grant got in front of me and led the way. The goat stared at us from the sidelines. After a short distance, I heard a noise behind me. I turned and saw the goat trotting after me. I dropped to one knee and offered it a peanut. The goat approached and took the peanut from my hand. At this point, it looked like a medium-sized, spotlessly clean black goat with intelligent green eyes. It had absolutely no visible sex organs or scent.

After a few more peanuts, the goat nuzzled me aside and proceeded along the trail. It looked back to see if I were following.

"I think it wants to lead," I said to Grant. Grant stepped aside to allow the goat to pass, but the goat clearly wanted to be between us. We walked in silence for about a mile. It was getting dark. I said, "We're going to have to turn back soon. If the goat is still with us when that time comes, we're going to have to bring it home with us." Grant agreed.

Suddenly, the goat went past Grant and led us up a rise. We sat on a precipice in the waning light. I fed the goat water from my hands. It kept its distance from Grant and nestled beside me. As we rose to leave, the goat climbed a hill and looked down on me one more time, looking enormous before it disappeared into the brush.

Grant and I retraced our steps back to the car. I noted the peanut shells along the trail and the forest where I first saw the goat was still inverted sharply inward.

"Did we spend the past few hours with a goat, or was I hallucinating?" I asked.

"We definitely spent time with a goat."

"I'm going to call the forest service. I don't want that goat eaten by a bear."

It was late by the time we got home, so I called the forest service the next morning.

"Have there been any goat sightings on the Appalachian Trail lately, up by Neel's Gap?" I asked the ranger.

There was silence on the other end of the phone before the ranger replied, "I've been working the AT for twenty-five years, ma'am, and I'm very familiar with Neel's Gap. Nobody has ever reported a barnyard animal on the trail and I've never seen one myself. I would say you had a very special encounter." I could just picture him rolling his eyes.

That's when I got it into my head that I may have had an encounter with a satyr – although I was surely no wood nymph. I looked up deities on the Internet. That's when I learned that there is a type of satyr known as a Slavonic Ljeschi that lives in the woods and appears to change size. It's there to protect other animals and can tickle humans to death.

"Holy shit," I said. I tried to call Grant at work but he was tied up, so I called my mother and told her I had an encounter with a Slavonic Ljeschi.

"What?" she said. "You're involved with a Slavic lesbian?"

"No, I haven't become a lesbian. I ran into a goat in the woods and I believe it might be a form of satyr."

"You ran into a ghost? You're going to a Seder?"

"Are you having hearing difficulties today?" I asked. Why was I calling my mother anyway? She wasn't going to get it. "Never mind," I said. I needed to get to work anyway.

I met my client at a Starbuck's. Karl was an adventurous guy with the most intense green eyes. We talked business for a while, and then we talked about our weekends. He climbed a mountain with ropes and pitons. And, I had a close encounter with a goat on the AT.

Big, rugged Karl got up and ran from me yelling, "You are the spawn of Satan!"

That was a novel interpretation of my experience and it would be ironic because my father actually believed that he was the second coming of Christ (he did feel a strange vibration at Maimonides tomb).

Several years have passed. We've returned to Neel's Gap time and again, but the goat has not reappeared. We even took my parents for a hike there once. At the beginning of the trail, my mother asked a hiker who was leaving, "Did you see any goats in there?" The poor clueless hiker thought she said "ghosts" and fled to his car without responding.

Maybe the goat was a ghost, after all – a peanut-eating, water-guzzling, dimension-altering phantom. Or, maybe I was frolicking with a satyr. Or, maybe I actually am the spawn of Satan.

Or, maybe sometimes a goat is just a goat.

YAH MON

*Twenty-one years ago, my husband and I spent our honeymoon in Negril,
Jamaica where we got to run around naked with a bunch of strangers and have close
encounters with dangerous marine life and drug peddlers. We also had a wonderful time.
After all these years, I'm happy to say that our parts are still intact and we still love each
other – even with tan lines.*

NAKED IN NEGRIL

APRIL 2013

My husband, Grant, and I are celebrating our twenty-first anniversary
this April. We've actually been together for twenty-six years, but who's
counting?

We didn't really know where to go for our honeymoon so we went to
see our local travel agent. Don turned out to be a real Jamaica freak.

The last time I had been to Jamaica was in 1976 and that was on a
familiarization tour of newly-developed Negril. I was a New York-based
travel agent and just learning my way around the world. Negril was a real
eye-opener.

Just for the sake of background, the first time I was in Negril I shared a
room in a brand-new hotel with a co-worker. Trudy was in her thirties and
had three children and lots of teeth and was lots of fun.

I'll give you a quick Trudy story. She and I went to a cocktail party
thrown by the Jamaican Tourist Board one night and got blitzed beyond all
human recognition on various rum concoctions. As we staggered around in
the wee hours, we discovered that we couldn't locate our room in the
sprawling complex. We managed to find our way to the front desk in our
long, flowery dresses but the night clerk refused to help us for some reason.
I still don't know why.

At any rate, off we went down the beach where we were soon pursued by really large land crabs. That was a fairly nightmarish experience so we broke into what turned out to be the honeymoon suite where we wrapped ourselves in bedspreads and shower curtains and went to sleep.

The next morning, deeply hung over, we needed to find our way back to the front desk again where a more reasonable clerk took pity on us and led us to our room. In the coming days, I ended up taking a "familiarization tour" of a local Jamaican Tourist Board agent who wasn't crazy about American women because he thought they were shameless sluts with no culture. I also accidentally ate a delicious plateful of goat covered in ants. When I started screaming, the host said, "Why are you screaming? They're only ants."

Okay, enough about the good old days.

Or, more about more recent good old days.

Grant and I flew to Jamaica from Atlanta in the spring of 1992. We arrived in Montego Bay and took a bus to Negril, where Don had booked us a room in a very exclusive all-inclusive resort.

After we were warmly welcomed and checked in, a lovely local walked us to our room. The further we walked the more naked the people on the beach got.

"What is this? I asked. "We didn't sign up for a nude beach." Not that there's anything wrong with that.

"We knew you were newly-weds so we just naturally assumed you would want to be on the nude beach," said the lovely local.

I turned to my husband and said, "We can stay here, if you'd like, but there's no way in hell I'm going to run around naked in this sun and burn my tatas off." I don't think Grant heard me. He may have been preoccupied with the other tatas already exposed and dangling in the breeze on the beach.

I must say, ten minutes later we were both cavorting nakedly on the hot sand. It was my first public nudity experience. Nobody seemed to give a damn. They were at home in their bodies – and, frankly, some of their bodies were the size of homes. With the amount of food being consumed on the all-you-can-eat buffet, we learned the true meaning of "bellying up to the bar."

Since this was a brave first for me, I decided to try another brave first: snorkeling. In the nude.

My first challenge was trying to find a snorkel mask that would fit my child-size face. I actually look a little like an anteater. The guy who was renting snorkel gear finally gave me a mask for a two-year-old – a human one. But, he didn't show me how to put it on.

So, while Grant was out flopping around in the Caribbean, I was standing naked in two inches of water struggling to put on my mini-mask.

A naked gentleman onshore noticed my difficulty. He got up from his beach chair and came flailing toward me, probably with all of the best of intentions. He extended his hand (glad he didn't extend his snorkel) and introduced himself. He was from L.A. Of course, he was from L.A.

At any rate, he did manage to cram me into my mask and then he went bouncing back to his beach chair.

My next brave challenge was putting my face in the water with hard contact lenses on. I've been wearing hard contacts since I've been twelve and had never submerged my face and opened my eyes. I did so with trepidation – and wonder of wonders! – the lenses stayed in my head and I was able to see quite well. A whole new world opened up for me in the sea – and, while it was beautiful, it pretty much kept me out of the ocean for the next twenty years. I'll tell you why (now that I've got your attention).

I went paddling down to where Grant was and put my head in the water. When I emerged, I said, "Sweetie, I think we're surrounded by barracudas." He said, "What are you talking about? There are no barracudas here. Those are needlefish – gars. They won't hurt you." And, once again, his head disappeared under water.

He popped up rather abruptly. "Holy shit," he began (never a good way to start). "We're surrounded by barracudas!", at which time we both started swimming furiously to shore covering our private parts. I actually put one hand on top of the other – because one of my hands wore a very shiny diamond ring that I was afraid would excite the barracudas – and I cupped them on my udders, using them like rudders – and kicked like a madman. The guy in the beach chair was no longer there or I'm sure he would've come running to assist us. Somehow.

We had two other snorkeling experiences that day. In one, Grant and I took out a kayak and paddled our way to a private cove where we, once again, leaped into the water with our parts hanging out. That's when we found the school of lobsters. Jesus.

So, later that day, we got on a snorkeling boat and visited a coral reef decked out in hazmat suits. Only kidding about the hazmat suits – but we were no longer naked.

Our resort was really pretty tame, especially compared to the resort across the street where people were freely fornicating in the lobby. At our resort, people were generally very well behaved – except for one woman who mistook our resort for the joint across the street and attempted to blow her husband in the communal hot tub without drowning. I, happily, missed this display. Grant caught the show, however, and reported it to me in detail. Who needed to go hot-tubbing in that heat, anyway? Not I.

The same woman and her husband showed up to the "come as you are" pajama party in which most people, apparently, slept in the nude. Big surprise. Grant wore one of my slips that came down to his upper thighs

49

and I wore a black lace teddy, which, for some reason, was more embarrassing than showing up in nothing at all. The hot tub blow-job queen showed up naked, of course, and attempted to pole dance. She learned that this hotel had its limits. She was told that only clothed people could slime around on the pole. Go figure. So, she mounted her sizable husband instead.

Grant won a hat for having the best "sleeping outfit" – don't ask where he put his room key – and played the piano for the writhing masses.

The resort mostly housed straight couples but there were a few gay guys in the mix. They fell in love with my husband and ran after him, squealing "Oh, piano man!" for the rest of the trip. I could've been dipped in chocolate. They only had eyes for him – especially after he got his WASPy hair corn-rowed. My Isro gives me a natural Rasta look – but, I had a couple of braids and beads added for fun. And, orange nail polish. And, I still got ignored. Blame it on the bossa nova. Or, in this case, the reggae.

When we weren't running around naked with strangers, we spent quiet times alone. It was our honeymoon, after all. Unfortunately, my husband used to look like a drug runner, which was a real come-on to the local drug peddlers. Every day, Grant would sit out on our private dock and meditate. And every day, a little boat would pull up to the dock with a couple of guys trying to interest him in their vast array of heroin, cocaine and ganja. Each day, Grant sat there like he was made of wood, but the boatmen wouldn't be ignored. Man, were they persistent.

So, the stoned security guard finally chased them away. He befriended my husband. They had long, philosophical conversations and the guard gave Grant a gift. It was a talking stick that he wanted Grant to carry back to the States.

Grant kept the stick for one night and got terribly sick from its energy. Who knows what was buried inside of it – or was slathered on top of it. He had to figure out a way to return the stick without offending the security guard. He finally told the man that he wasn't strong enough to carry his stick. I hope he said stick. The man took it back with a sad smile but I sense we avoided a long jail sentence in a Jamaican prison.

So – that was twenty-one years ago. We've had a couple of other public nudity experiences since then, but none as colorful as the ones on our honeymoon – and not as dangerous. I mean, what is likely to bite your genitals off at a Japanese health spa? Koi? I don't think so.

So, happy anniversary to my loving husband who looks even better now than he did on our honeymoon. I bet he'd still fit into my slip.

MI CASA ES SU CASA

My husband and I moved to Santa Fe, New Mexico about eight years ago and we love it here. When we first moved into our house, though, I suspect it was infested with fairies and poltergeists. I exorcised the little monsters with a few years of nonstop screaming and running amok – so it's safe to visit now. Just disregard the geckos in the guest room shower and the tarantulas doing pushups on the flagstone patio. I understand they're harmless. On the other hand, step away from the adorable bunnies – they'll give you bubonic plague. Sweet dreams.

HAUNTED HACIENDA

MAY 2013

Call me crazy, but the minute I moved into my new house in Santa Fe I knew that it contained at least one fairy, and I'm not talking about my husband who regularly flits around the living room doing tai chi maneuvers. To have a fairy in a house means that objects mysteriously disappear and strange things happen. Hmmm – maybe I am talking about my husband. But, I certainly couldn't blame him for the weirdness that occurred in the first few months we moved into our house because he worked and lived elsewhere for a while, leaving me to battle the fairies alone – with the aid of various day workers.

First of all, all of my appliances were infested with fairies – or maybe poltergeists. I'm not kidding. It all started when I tried to open my refrigerator for the first time. I managed to get food into the freezer all right but when I went to put my other groceries away, the door refused to open. I tugged at it for a while and then started to look for child locks. There were none. The door finally opened on its own – mysteriously. I could just hear the fairies giggling away. At least, they didn't hide my lamb chops. Yet.

I went through this exercise for a couple of weeks before calling Larry the appliance man. He came with his little toolkit. I explained my problem. He sneered at me and suggested that maybe I wasn't strong enough to open the fridge door. I sneered back and invited him to give it a shot. I had secretly opened the freezer door just before Larry arrived. He yanked the fridge around the kitchen for a while and the door stayed glued shut – until it opened on its own. I told him I thought it had something to do with the freezer. But, secretly, I knew it was fairies we were dealing with.

Larry asked if I would mind if he inserted a narrow tube into a small hole at the base of the refrigerator and I told him to have at it. He seemed to think this action would break some kind of vapor seal. I stepped back and let Larry violate my fridge, after which he shut the door. I challenged him to try to reopen it, but try as he might, it stayed shut until it opened on its own. Larry took a new approach.

"Do you mind if I take this power tool and drill behind your gasket?" he asked. He held his tool up for me to see. It was impressive.

"Isn't that going to render my refrigerator as energy efficient as a grass hut in the Yukon?" I asked.

Larry didn't know, but I told him to drill away. I held my ears. When he was finished, he shut the door and attempted to reopen it. Once again, the fridge thwarted Larry – at which time he said, "Ma'am, you've got the tightest gasket I've ever seen." Now, *that's* a remark every woman over eighteen wants to hear. Nevertheless, I knew at that juncture that Larry wasn't going to be able to handle my problem with the refrigerator. I would deal with the fridge on its own terms: open the freezer, close the freezer, wait one minute, open the fridge door. Voila. I'm a refrigerator psychologist. And I'm onto how those fairies operate.

Two weeks later, I had to call Larry again. This time, there was something screwy going on with the oven. There didn't seem to be a light in there. I called a friend who I knew had the same appliance and asked, "Is it possible that this oven doesn't come with a light?" "No, you idiot," she replied. Damn it. I was going to have to have another service call. Good thing all the appliances were under warranty.

So, Larry came back with his toolkit and peered into the oven. "The light's not coming on," he said.

"That's correct. That's why I called you."

Larry proceeded to yank the oven out of the wall, at which time there was a loud explosion and Larry lay on the floor gyrating like he'd been Tasered. Once he stopped quivering, he said, "The electricity isn't connected properly. Where's your circuit breaker?" Gee – he probably should have asked that question before he yanked the oven out of the wall. Nevertheless, he did manage to get a light on in the oven without killing himself.

The next call wasn't to Larry. It was to the builder because only he knew why the phone wires didn't extend to the exterior of the house and where they might be hidden. The builder sent over a man who said, "I can fix it but I don't have my tool. Plus, it's Friday and I only work until noon." I block out what I had to do to get him to find his tool and fix my problem that day because more perils lay ahead.

The builder had to send over a spelunking expert because I couldn't locate wiring for the TV. Turns out, the TV wires were buried in our beautiful diamond plaster walls. And the radiant heating system wasn't working in the family room. One service guy came over and told me he would need to use a stick of dynamite to fix that problem – fortunately, a brighter fellow who didn't speak any English had a much easier solution that didn't require blowing up the house. He switched out two wires in the utility room and our problem was solved.

One night, I thought I would relax with a little music but one of the stereo speakers was making a frightening sound. So, the builder sent over Chris the electrician. Chris took one look into the offending speaker and started nodding sagely.

"What is it, a crimped wire?" I asked.

"No," he said. "A mouse ate your woofer."

"Say what?"

"A mouse ate your woofer."

"What do you mean, a mouse ate my woofer? Who are you, Dr. Seuss?"

"All of these houses are riddled with rodents," he said. "Would you like me to put a bull snake in your wall?"

"Say what?" I squeaked again, probably sounding like the mouse who ate my woofer.

"If I put a bull snake in your wall," Chris explained, "it will keep your rodent population under control."

"What if he runs out of food?"

"Don't worry. He won't."

"Holy shit. No, I don't want a bull snake in my wall. What I want is a plane ticket back to civilization. Is there any other solution?"

"I can put some steel wool in there."

"Do that."

As I walked him out, he started nodding again.

"Now what?" I asked.

"You've got goat heads."

"Oh, for the love of Mike. I know I'm not as young as I used to be but surely I don't have a goat head yet."

"Goat heads are toxic weeds," he explained. "You need a flame thrower to get rid of them."

"Oh, that's just fucking terrific."

Where was my husband when I needed him? He was back in civilization, that's where – if you consider Atlanta civilization (and I do). I was going to kill him when he got home.

Unfortunately, I wasn't finished with Larry the appliance man yet. I should have just rented him a room. I would have rented Chris the electrician a room but he told me he was a former violent felon, recently released from prison, where he found Jesus. I assume he wasn't talking about his cellmate.

This time, it was the wine cooler. It was rusting in front of my eyes. I don't know what Larry did to it, but it's still rusting – and still working, miraculously. He did agree to replace our outdoor gas grill, however, because someone had turned it on without removing the packaging and the packaging had become one with the stainless steel it was housed in.

How did that happen? Either the grill was turned on when a realtor threw a party at the house during a home show, complete with mariachi band, before we bought it, or the fucking fairies turned the grill on. I haven't ruled them out. Either way, the appliance was toast.

You don't want to get me started on the leaky roof, the disintegrating stucco, the fragile flagstone, the crumbling asphalt driveway, the poorly-engineered shower stall, the glacially-slow Internet service, the ever-shifting desert sands that crack your walls and floors, the pinholes in the copper piping, the perpetually rolling carpets or the closets that go sproinging off their hinges.

And, how can I possibly forget the time I came into the kitchen and watched what I thought was my husband having an epiphany? He stood looking upward toward the skylight, his arms outstretched. It was a beautiful sight until I realized it was snowing on his face.

One more thing – isn't there always one more thing? - once a year I go berserk from Miller moths who come in swarms to set themselves aflame in the lighting fixtures for a few weeks. My husband should probably videotape me battling them in my nightgown. I make every effort to keep them from self-immolating because once they set themselves (and the fixtures) on fire, the whole house smells like burnt broccoli. But, they insist on playing Buddhist monk anyway. I would say they, too, are fucking fairies but would fucking fairies set themselves aflame and become flaming fucking fairies? No – they're too smart for that.

Okay, I've stopped hyperventilating. By now, we've been here for a while. Everything's been repaired or replaced and we've made our peace with the fairies and poltergeists and even the building inspector who didn't bother to actually inspect our house before we moved into it. In fact, we love the house, quirks and all. We've been told by several people who are in a position to know that we have one of the best built houses in this town and certainly one of the most peaceful.

I think it's finally safe to say, "Y'all come. Welcome to Guatemala.

MY GOYISHE PAPA?

My father came from a religious Jewish home and he practiced his faith – well, faithfully. However, at the end of his life, he made a strange admission. Or, maybe it was a joke. Just to be on the safe side, we do both the tarantella and the hora – and maybe a jig – at bar mitzvahs and christenings. You never know.

THAT EXPLAINS EVERYTHING!

JUNE 2013

I never doubted that I was Jewish, until very recently. Why would I have doubted it? My great-grandparents were all bearded and looked like Chassidic rabbis – even the women! So, why would I ever question my background? I'll tell you why.

As my father was approaching the end of his life, hospice workers kept coming into his room to torment him with idiotic questions like, "Where were you born?" and "What day is this?" I realize they were just trying to determine if he was having issues with dementia but, really, at that point, what difference did it make?

My father answered most of the questions correctly – which is why we were a little confused when he was asked what his religion was and he said, "Catholic." Who knew (nu?)? A lot of people (not Jewish people, of course - they can immediately identify me as a landsman) ask me if I'm Italian, French or Irish. Maybe I am! Pick one!

I think my father was having a little laugh at the expense of the hospice workers. Either that, or I come from a long line of Catholic rabbis. Oy vey.

When my father passed, my mother started spending a few months out of the year in a senior living facility in Colorado. She spends the other months of her year in South Florida, a real hotbed of Christianity.

One day, she told me she was attending church services. I told her I thought that was great.

"What denomination?" I asked.

"Let me check the program," she said. "It's Gospel. I really like singing the songs."

"How do you know the words?"

"They're right there in the book. But they're all about Jesus."

"No kidding. Are you getting something out of the sermons?"

"Oh, yes. They move me to tears. Plus, the pastor is very handsome. He always gives me a big greeting and remembers my name."

I was so happy that my mother was having a spiritual experience. I remember when she and I and my brother got thrown out of temple for cracking up when the rabbi said, "Abraham tied his ass to a tree and walked forty miles." Now, that's a pretty amazing feat. My father was covering his face in shame in the choir loft while *our* asses were being ushered out of the sanctuary.

One time, I visited my mother in Colorado and asked her if she were going to services that day. She told me she wasn't because she was pissed at the pastor.

"Why are you pissed at the pastor?" I asked. "What did the pastor do to piss you off?" I nearly spit my teeth out twice just asking those questions.

"He lied to us."

"The pastor lied to you? About what?"

"He said the piano lady wasn't there because she was stuck in traffic."

"So – what's wrong with that?"

"She was in Las Vegas."

"Well, maybe she was stuck in traffic in Las Vegas."

"That's what he told us afterward," my mother said.

Maybe my mother will return to services, after all.

That works for me because my family is a mixed bag as far as religion goes anyway and has been since my father's generation.

What difference does it make, in the grand scheme of things?

My mother once caught the cantor from our temple slipping bacon into his shopping cart. It was one of those awkward moments. But, big deal. What? Jews don't eat pork in Chinese restaurants every Sunday? Give me a break.

And now, if you'll excuse me, I'm going to have a matzo brei with ham.

I'VE GROWN A-COSTUMED TO MY CLOTHES

They say that clothes make the man – or woman. I think of clothes as costumes. When you put something on, you can choose to blend in or stand out. You have an opportunity to make a personal statement every day and my statement is: This is who I choose to be today.

DEAD MAN'S PANTS

JULY 2013

Some years ago – and, by some, I mean thirty – I was working as a public relations manager for a high-tech corporation in Atlanta. My boss had a wife who was gathering information for a book on professional image and she wanted me to ghostwrite it for her. She invited me out to lunch to discuss the issue. I was trying to be so polite that I cut a plum with a knife. Unfortunately, the plum flew across the table and landed in her well-dressed lap.

"You want me to write a book on professional image?" I said. "I look like the aftermath of a Gypsy wagon explosion."

"Not write it," she said, looking at my wild hair and magenta broom skirt with amusement, "just ghostwrite it – and, make it funny."

It's already funny," I said. "Plus, I can write the whole book in a single paragraph: Women in business, cut your hair and wear gray or navy suits with knee-length skirts, tailored blouses, black pumps with a two-inch heel and simple jewelry; men, do the same thing – without the pumps and skirts (unless you're Scottish).

"It would be a short book without photos," she admitted. Nevertheless, she was forming a successful seminar business and the book would certainly expand her influence in the "dress-for-success" industry. I suggested a "dress-for-distress" chapter – now, *that* was something I could

58

write about – but, she knew I was kidding.

"Let me go ask my boss," I said.

My boss merely said, "Are you working for me or are you working for my wife?"

"I guess I'm working for you," I said.

Frankly, I don't know which way it would've worked out better. The wife found another ghostwriter and the book was a big hit. I can't complain about my career path, though – and nobody seemed to care what the hell I wore as long as I got the job done. I always looked professional. I merely resisted uniformity.

I always had my own eclectic style and there were certain items I simply couldn't put on. For example, I got thrown out of the Brownies when I was six because I refused to wear the stupid brown beanie and ankle socks. Socks, in general, don't do it for me. I also don't like khaki, short-sleeved shirts and Bermuda shorts.

I think being persnickety about dress may run in the family. I have one niece who insisted upon going to her great-grandpa's birthday naked (I should point out that she was two at the time) and I've never seen her own daughter in anything other than fairy dresses. The kid was born with an aversion to pants. And her big brother is partial to formal attire. It's not every day that you see a seven-year-old in a smoking jacket and monocle. These are my kind of kids.

Some years back – and by some, I mean fifteen – I began to enjoy shopping at consignment stores. It was just so much fun going into a store and never knowing what you were going to find. I have a peculiar size, which makes it easier to stumble into almost-new, interesting-looking garb that nobody else would even consider. I would say that, at this point, half of my wardrobe is new and the other half is used.

I live in Santa Fe, New Mexico where celebrities and other wealthy individuals buy very expensive clothing, decide they don't want it and bring it to consignment shops. Their loss is definitely my gain. I may not wear their discarded clothing either, but my closet looks like a work of art.

I recently bought my husband four pairs of jeans at a consignment store. At two dollars and fifty cents a pair, they fit better than any jeans he's ever worn in his life. Either some body double bought the farm and left my husband with four pairs of lightly-worn thirty-six by thirty fours or some rich guy had more jeans than he knew what to do with and got rid of a few. Maybe they belonged to Gene Hackman.

Some people, like my brother, would be grossed out at the idea of wearing some dead guy's pants – or even some live guy's pants. I say that unless the guy was actually wearing the pants when he died (or unless the pants somehow killed him – which would be a clear indication that they had bad mojo), I don't see any problem in wearing recycled clothing. It's like recycling organs – why not have a part of you live on?

To me, garments have a story all their own. I may keep an article of clothing forever simply because it reminds me of who I was with when I bought it. I kept an angora sweater my grandmother bought me at the Alexander's department store in Queens when I was twelve until it got devoured by moths last year – and, even then, I was reluctant to part with it. I have my mother's mink hat, which I will never wear. I have a few pairs of those corporate pumps that wheeled me around so many trade shows. And, I have several beautiful business suits adorning my guest room closet. I get to visit myself at different stages of life. Friends occasionally ask me for an article of my clothing and I couldn't be more flattered.

I have a new friend who is coming to visit me in September. She asked me what people wore in Santa Fe. I told her Spandex, but that's just me. People can wear a gunny sack and bunny ears in Santa Fe and nobody would give them a second glance. I've seen one woman here who walks around town dressed like a witch, complete with broom and curly-toed shoes. It's my kind of town. On the other hand, it's good to have something other than overalls lying around in case you're summoned to jury duty or a funeral.

And, speaking of funerals, a few years back my friend Dorothy and I went to an estate sale. The estate sale was for a recently-deceased woman whose initials were "ASS." We saw the inscription on her bathrobe. We were wondering if there was another bathrobe that said, "TITS." Unfortunately, there wasn't. It would've been fun having both. But, having somebody's strange, dead "ASS" hanging in the closet all by itself – not so much.

My old boss was also a big fan of having his initials inscribed on his belongings. All of his shirts bore the insignia "JVP" and I wish I had one hanging in my closet. He died eight years ago but his wife parted with him and his clothing many years before that.

Maybe I'm glad that I chose to work for him, after all.

PLEASE LEAVE ME A MASSAGE

Okay, so this is a simple story about self-indulgence. I don't get mani-pedis. I don't go to fancy hair salons. I don't pay retail, if I can avoid it. And, I'm very low-maintenance. But, I do enjoy the occasional massage and the pre- or post-soak that sometimes goes with it. And, if I enjoy it, there's a story in it. So, here it is.

RUB ME TENDER

SEPTEMBER 2013

I work out a lot and by "work out" I mean Zumba, yoga and Pilates. I don't pump a whole lot of iron because it bores me witless. I do pump my own body weight several times a week (e.g., yoga pushups) and I hope that keeps me from disintegrating anytime soon. I'm probably pretty fit, but I frequently feel like I've been run over by a train. Because of this, I go for a massage every couple of months, or so. And, I soak in hot tubs, with or without Jacuzzi jets.

I've had my share of very interesting massage experiences. The very first one I ever got was around thirty-five years ago. I was in Santa Fe, New Mexico with my first husband. We were walking through a hotel corridor and noticed a shop that was advertising massages for twenty-five dollars. I decided to try it.

The massage therapist was a Sikh who lived in an ashram in Espanola. His name was Gurushawan and he was very tall and thin. To tell you the truth, he looked a little like Osama bin Laden – but, at the time, I just saw him as a lanky guy with a dark beard and a white turban.

I don't think a massage table was involved. I seem to recall lying on the blanketed floor and talking a lot. Gurushawan worked on me for two-and-a-half hours and my neck felt great for five years after that. It was that therapeutic. Of course, my ex was wondering what the hell was going on in there for so long, but he was soon to find out. He was Gurushawan's next customer – but he only got an hour.

On my forty-sixth birthday, I got massaged by a nice twenty-two-year-old man at a day spa in Atlanta. At one point, while he was rubbing my forearm, a flame shot out and knocked him across the room. I damn near fell off the massage table.

"What the hell was that?" he squealed, which sounded kind of funny with the New Age music playing in the background. "I think I have a lot of electricity in my body," I said, as calmly as possible. I mean, how calm can you be when flames are coming out of your body? Electricity? I'd be good to have around in a blackout, in case someone runs out of matches.

Now, I'm living in Santa Few with my current husband, Grant. Santa Fe is crawling with massage therapists. They work out of spas, hotels, casitas – some even carry a table in their car and work on you in the privacy of your own home. Some of them are very good. Some are very chatty. Some prefer to work in silence, although the New Age music hasn't gone out of style yet.

On a recent anniversary, Grant and I went to a Japanese spa in Santa Fe for deluxe (i.e., insanely expensive) massages and a soak in the communal tub.

We had tried couples massages before and opted against it this time because – let's face it – with a massage, you really want it to be all about you. So, our anniversary massages took place in separate quarters – a girl for him, a boy for me. All I wanted to do was lose the pain in my neck (where was Gurushawan when I needed him? I suspect he moved back to Rochester, New York and became an accountant, or something, but I digress…).

Grant told me his masseuse was a skilled reflexologist and worked in silence. My masseur, on the other hand, was a raving maniac in a beret who squashed my breasts into the table while he worked out his hostilities. Over the hour-and-a half I spent on the table, I heard the entire story of his sad life. He had a wife once and she left him and he cried a river. Then, the truth came out. He's was as gay as a party hat. Unfortunately, his male partner also left him. Recently. Maybe that morning. I may have grunted sympathetically – or maybe I felt one of my ribs break. At any rate (I think it was two hundred and twenty dollars), his name was Gilbert – but he pronounced it Gil-Bear. I'll bet he wasn't even French. I felt like charging him two hundred and twenty dollars and suggesting he get a prescription for Prozac. But, I didn't.

After getting manhandled by Gil-Bear for a full ninety minutes (and not a second more), I really needed some R&R, so I headed to the communal tub, which was right outside the women's bathhouse. At the time, I was not accustomed to public nudity – except for the nude beach we ended up on during our honeymoon many years before. I guess it wasn't really all that shocking in either context. Grant was waiting for me in his usual post-massage state of stupefaction. He hadn't taken his robe off yet, which was probably just as well. In his current condition, he may have stumbled and drowned in the cold plunge.

There were three naked guys sunning themselves around the tub. They looked like self-conscious turtles. I made a beeline for the sauna, where three other naked guys were baking themselves like potatoes. I suspected they were all busy checking each other out, so I took off my robe and sprawled on a ledge. Nobody looked. It was hotter than blazing hell in there. I got out before my nipples burst into flame and went back to the edge of the hot tub, where Grant was blissfully snoozing in a low wooden chair with his parts falling out of his robe. Little did he know. And, I didn't tell him! And, it didn't matter anyhow.

I noticed there was a Teutonic-looking couple in the hot tub that could have come leaping out of Leipzig. He was a big, muscular guy with a crew cut. My ex had a theory about big, muscular men. He thought they all had wienies the size of French fries. He, of course, was a very skinny guy. By the time I looked to test his theory, Adolph's wiener schnitzel was underwater and his wife's sizable thigh was on top of it. She looked like one of the seven maids-a-milking. I left before they start singing arias from Wagner.

No self-respecting Japanese spa would be without a koi pond and this one was no exception. Grant was still napping so I slipped off to look at the koi and sip lemon water. I bent over the pond and the koi come swimming up to me with their mouths open. There was a big sign in front of the pond that said, "Do Not Feed the Koi" and all I had was lemon water so I pet them instead. They looked disappointed. It was time to go. The massages and the hot tub and the sauna and the lemon water and the disappointed koi added up to three million dollars.

Nowadays, I divide my time, unequally, between Santa Fe and Atlanta. In Atlanta, where I spend the smaller percentage of my time, I occasionally treat myself to a massage at a day spa where they specialize in trying to sell you health and beauty products while they work on you for exactly sixty minutes. Conversely, I have two massage therapists I go to in Santa Fe. One works out of her house and one works out of his casita. They both massage me for at least two hours apiece (no, not at the same time). She is a comedian when she's not massaging people – and, sometimes while she's massaging people. He's a building contractor when he's not massaging people and he's capable of hauling me around like a big stack of cordwood. Both are excellent.

I would tell you the names of my massage therapists in Santa Fe, but they're MINE! ALL MINE! However, if you should happen to run into

Gurushawan out there and he's not an accountant, get down on the floor immediately and request a massage. Do it even if he is an accountant! He's probably still the best there is.

SHORT AND SWEET

Most people who know me know that my baking repertoire is pretty limited. I have a few specialties that give me an excuse to drink in the afternoon like Julia Child while I combine butter and brown sugar and flour in a big bowl and plunge my hands into the mix like a child in a mud bath. But the outcome is always satisfying and it makes the house smell like heaven. How better to usher in the holidays?

EAT MY COOKIES

NOVEMBER 2013

As holiday season approaches, I am reminded of a tradition in my old neighborhood in Duluth, Georgia – the annual cookie exchange hosted by my next-door neighbor, Anne Marie. The first invitation struck up a little apprehension in my heart because, while I was happy to be included, I was not a cookie person. In fact, I had bad cookie memories ever since my childhood next-door neighbor refused to buy the Girl Scout cookies I was peddling because I was still a Brownie. She insisted that I refer to the cookies as brownies instead of Girl Scout cookies, which I couldn't relate to because there wasn't a brownie in the lot – just thin mints and Samoas and other weird-sounding crap. What did I know? I was six. And, I got thrown out of the Brownies, anyway, for refusing to wear the dumb-ass beanie. I never did become a Girl Scout. Where the hell was I? Oh, yes – the cookie exchange.

In preparation for Christmas, about a dozen women would congregate in Anne Marie's living room with baskets full of beautifully-decorated holiday cookies – delicate confections in the shapes of Christmas trees and Santa Clauses and glossy little rum balls. The women were all raised around holiday cookies. In my childhood home, we had Oreos, Fig Newtons and Mallomars, holidays included. The only dessert my mother prepared was

My-T-Fine chocolate pudding. And she occasionally opened a can of fruit cocktail.

From what I hear, my grandmother used to bake rugelach. I would've enjoyed hearing the women try to pronounce rugelach but who brings rugelach to a Christmas cookie exchange? Not me – but mostly because I didn't inherit my grandmother's rugelach genes.

I should mention that all of the women who came to the exchange had children. I was eccentric to the neighborhood. All I had was a cat and he preferred broccoli to cookies. Still, I wanted to do my part so I bought a cookbook. I didn't really want to get involved with cookie cutters and sugary sparkles and multi-colored sprinkles and rolling pins – although I did get a rolling pin as a bridal shower gift once. I let my ex have it in the divorce settlement. He recovered eventually.

I was always a bit of a sculptor and the cookbook had recipes that allowed you to shape cookies by hand. That sounded like a plan. I went shopping for ingredients and a big bowl and figured – how hard can it be? I threw everything together and started making shapes out of what felt like clay with nuts. I didn't think anything would come out looking like Rudolph the Red-Nosed Reindeer but I thought – with a little luck – it would come out looking like a nice, round ornament. Yeah, like something you would hang on the gargantuan tree at Rockefeller Center.

The recipe instructed me to take my batter and roll it into really small balls. When I laid them on the cookie sheet, they looked far too small so I took liberties with the recipe. Hey, I'm a nonconformist. I don't need some book telling me how big my balls should be. I made nice, big balls – so what if there was only enough batter for two cookies? I could always make up another batch. I made up several batches. They smelled delicious while they were baking. I was really going to wow those Bentley Place women!

Well, those big balls expanded into really gigantic golden hockey pucks in the oven. It was too late to do anything about it. I loaded my cookies into a suitcase and hauled them over to Anne Marie's and damn near got a hernia. They each weighed about four-hundred pounds. The women watched in amazement as I set them out on the dining room table on a really large platter that dwarfed all those dainty Christmas plates. The women politely tasted my contribution to the exchange – all twelve shared a half a cookie and declared it very tasty. They broke the other half into a million pieces to share with their families – maybe.

I wanted to do better the next time. I knew I could make edible cookies. They just needed to be edible to people who were smaller than King Kong. So, I decided that following the recipe was a good idea.

That's when I stumbled into a recipe that someone had pilfered from Neiman Marcus and circulated on the Internet. It could've been a recipe for napalm, for all I knew, but it did contain ingredients like chocolate and walnuts and oatmeal – and the cookies were to be hand-shaped and I was an old hand at that – so I decided to pilfer it myself. I would make a few changes – because I can't help myself – but I would keep the balls small. And – voila! – I baked the best cookies ever. People have been putting in requests for them ever since and I never make them the same way twice. My husband is addicted to them altogether – I have a special, secret recipe for him. And, they are cookies for all seasons.

But, in the event I'm ever invited to another Christmas cookie exchange, I also bake a mean pecan puff. They're finished in snowy confectioner's sugar, are as light as fairy wings and would do Santa proud.

THE SKY IS FALLING!

I hate to fall prey to all the doomsayers out there but it's hard to be optimistic when the world seems to be going to hell in a handbasket. I would rather not get blasted back into the Stone Age – before fur was faux – but, when are we going to stop destroying our planet? Getting beamed up to the mothership is starting to sound like a good idea. Except for the probes.

THE HIDDEN CHICKEN

MAY 2014

Remember those old family vacations where you ended up drowsing in the back seat of the car wearing Mickey Mouse ears and a dazed expression? You don't? Well, I don't either. By the time my family made it out to Disneyland I was fourteen and wouldn't be caught dead in rodent attire. But, that's not the point of this story. The point is that, in the not-too-distant past, we may have been bored to death on a road trip but we were rarely afraid of actual death at the avenging hands of Mother Nature. I don't think I pissed her off personally – although I'm sure I'm guilty of some offense just because I live and breathe – but, I'm feeling very vulnerable to her wrath nonetheless.

We're all vulnerable and Mother seems to really have it in for the United States these days. When my husband and I were planning a road trip recently, I had to ask, "Do you want to go toward wildfires, mudslides, earthquakes, tsunamis and radioactive seafood or would you prefer tornados, hurricanes, floods, snow and baseball-sized hail?

I have to admit, when I went on that family vacation at fourteen, we did get stuck in a sandstorm in the Painted Desert, but that was only after my scofflaw mother smuggled artifacts out of the Petrified Forest in her bra. In a Karmic sense, for every action there's a reaction. It's clear that we have committed terrible actions to be in the mess we're in right now. And, even though I righteously returned my mother's pilfered slivers of wood to the Petrified Forest in my own bra forty years later, it was too late.

Perhaps we should follow in our friends' footsteps and head out of the country altogether – but what with flights disappearing off the face of the earth and diseases like polio making a comeback in foreign lands, I think we'll probably remain in New Mexico and take our chances with the aliens.

I am afraid of things I can't control because – well, because I'm a control freak and who can control Mother? Not me.

I was recently lying on a massage table schmoozing with my New-Age therapist, who's an old hippie from northern California. I told him, "We're getting ready to head west."

"Hmmm," he said. "When are you going?"

"May."

"I hope it's early May," he said ominously. "The Pacific Ring of Fire has been activated. The end of the world is near."

"Oh, for the love of Mike," I mumbled into the face cradle (or whatever you call those things). "You guys have been talking about the end of the world for ages."

"This time it's for real," he said. "I've been consulting my gurus. The end of time predicted in the Mayan calendar was intentionally off by a couple of years to give people time to realize the error of their ways before they got snuffed out."

"Yes, the ancient Mayans were very sophisticated that way," I said, adjusting my face. I was developing a pain in the neck that only Armageddon would cure.

I asked him if he thought I should cancel our trip and he just said, "I will pray for you."

So, here I am, preparing to take a road trip to the west coast with my husband (who believes that global warming has fucked us up but does not anticipate that we're going to get vaporized by a volcanic blast anytime soon) and I'm scared witless. I hate being such a chicken – it's a bad look for me – but with people praying for me and insurance companies jacking up the deductible on my homeowner's policy, I'm really afraid that something huge is going to happen.

Times were better when road trips were mostly adventurous ("Grand Canyon? What Grand Canyon? Where are the boys?"); sometimes inventive ("Hey, let's throw Mom into the Grand Canyon!"); and usually safe ("Get your mother away from that cliff and stop feeding those bears marshmallows!"). But, those days appear to be over. Now, I'm afraid we'll fall off the Pacific Coast Highway or go down the drain in the middle of the Great Basin.

If I survive this trip, I will be heading to Atlanta next, where I may be required to carry a gun. Wonder if I can shoot my way out of a thunderstorm.

In reality, the scariest part of this upcoming trip will probably be inhaling a friend's second-hand smoke. Cigarettes. Now, that's something that really freaks me out.

HOLDING ON

I don't lose people easily or enthusiastically. I choose to deepen relationships rather than marginalize them. And, I have a strong sense of place – an appreciation for what makes my heart beat; something that brings back my youth. Some call it ghost fever. I call it love.

GHOST FEVER

JULY 2014

I moved to Santa Fe, NM exactly nine years ago and, while life here is exciting and rich, I'm still pining for my home in Atlanta. I have to admit, I missed New York and Boston when I left there, too – but this time, I feel like I've left a lover behind.

I don't know what the hell is wrong with me. It's not like I'm dying to arm myself to go to the grocery store (more on the gun issue in a minute). That's not what I like about the South.

At any rate (a dollar three-eighty an hour?), I decided to speak to a counselor when I first got here because I had a few free sessions available to me and I figured, what the hey – might as well share my insanity with someone else.

My husband wasn't around to absorb my sadness – he deposited me in the desert and took off back to Atlanta so he could continue to be gainful. For several years, it was just me and the screaming coyotes and their cotton-tailed prey (which I was told carried bubonic plague – step away from the bunnies).

There were five therapists on my insurance list; three women and two men. The women were all focused on the plight of women in domestic violence situations. That wasn't me – unless you consider being stranded in the desert an act of violence.

One of the men on the list was the ex-husband of our realtor and I knew he was nuts. My last hope – a guy with a simple name like John Smith and a PhD – was willing to speak to me.

John Smith turned out to be Lakota Sioux on his father's side and Southern belle on his mother's side. He was raised by his paternal grandmother on the res. His real name was Running Moose and his PhD was in philosophy, not psychology.

When he was serious, John/Moose looked like Sitting Bull, who I think may have been a distant relation. When he smiled, he looked like Blanche DuBois, who may have also been a distant relation.

John/Moose was focused on the problems of gay, drug-addicted youths. He must've been surprised when I showed up. When I arrived at his door, I was greeted by a really frightening-looking pit bull named Sharkie. Sharkie keeled over as soon as he saw me.

"Are you afraid of dogs? John/Moose asked.

"Not this one," I said, pointing at the catatonic canine. "Is he okay?"

"He's narcoleptic," said John/Moose.

I stepped over the prone pooch and sat on the couch. John/Moose asked me, "What seems to be the problem?"

"I recently moved to Santa Fe from Atlanta and can't seem to settle into my new life here. I am actually yearning to be there."

I had never used the word "yearn" in a sentence before.

"How long have you been here?" he asked.

"About six months."

John/Moose gave me a dark look and informed me I had ghost fever. He explained, "On the res, when you experience a loss, you are given a limited amount of time to mourn. Once that period is up, you are expected to move on. If you can't move on, that's very serious business. Ghost fever is harshly dealt with."

"Oy vey," I said to myself.

John/Moose grabbed a handful of weeds he told me was sweet grass from his home in South Dakota and set one end of it on fire.

I prepared to be burned alive but, instead, John/Moose shook the smoking weeds about my person, chanting until Sharkie opened one eye and crawled into a dog tent in the corner of the room. This practice is called "smudging" and it's intended to ward off evil spirits.

I have a problem with smoke. It hurts my eyes, shuts down my nose and upsets my pancreas. Nevertheless, I sat through the entire exorcism with tolerance and high hopes. Was I going to be able to overcome ghost fever and say good-bye to my previous life? Especially since my current life was so stimulating?

No. It's been nine years and I still have ghost fever. John/Moose even tried turning a dead bird inside out to turn me around – I don't know what that practice is called – but it didn't work. Good thing I wasn't living on the res.

So, how do I handle my malady?

I go back to Atlanta once or twice or three times a year and stay a couple of weeks per visit. I usually stay in my own little room across from where I used to work out (L.A. Fitness). Sometimes I do an overnight with friends. I always visit the Chattahoochee River and walk in the lush woods all around it. I drink in all that's familiar and reconnect with people who are dear to me.

It would appear that my ghost fever is all about love. Seriously. If that's the case, it's a disease I don't want to recover from.

But it goes deeper than that. I moved to Atlanta in my twenties. I was young there. I grew up with people there for nearly thirty years. I was fifty-two years old when I moved to Santa Fe. I was never going to be young here. And I think that's what I'm mourning the most. I go back to Georgia and I'm young again, with the open heart of a girl.

Incidentally, I have moved on and I've never been more productive. That's rejuvenating. And, I have great friends here. Maybe someday I'll have ghost fever when I leave Santa Fe.

Having said that, I promised I would get back to the gun issue. Turns out that, like Georgia, half of New Mexico is also locked and loaded.

I was at a dinner party in Santa Fe one night schmoozing with a group of women. They were all discussing their Glocks and their Lugers and their Colt 45s and so forth. That really attracted my attention.

After getting an earful, I announced, "I don't have a firearm. If someone broke into my house in the middle of the night, all I'd be able to do is lie in bed and go, "Woof woof.""

My friend, Maxine, replied, "My husband gave me a gun eleven years ago but he never gave me any ammunition so if someone broke into my house, all I'd be able to do is point my big gun at him and go, "Woof woof.""

Now, that's speaking my language!

THE CALL OF THE KUCHALEIN

*Why would reasonably well-to-do families leave their suburban houses for a
bungalow or boarding house in the country? Well, we weren't always so well-to-do and,
at some point in our lives, we were leaving hot and squalid tenement apartments to spend
a summer among like-minded individuals in the Catskills, just as our ancestors had.
Want to know what "kuchalein" means? Read on..*

BUNGALOW BABY

APRIL 2015

On October 2, 2011, my husband and I flew down to Ft. Lauderdale
from Atlanta on a flight that originated in Albuquerque. We were flying
down in a hurry because my father was dying in a Delray Beach hospice. I
had spoken to him the night before and said to him, "You wait for me. I'll
be there tomorrow." Grant and I were on the next flight out of
Albuquerque, which left at six the next morning.

We almost didn't make it.

The first leg of the trip was okay, even though we were stuck in the very
last row of the plane. The second leg was a nightmare, with flight
attendants sprawling into the aisles and lots of people hyperventilating.
Oddly, before we began our galloping, life-threatening descent, I spotted a
woman walking down the aisle who looked very familiar to me. She was
looking at me and smiling broadly so I assumed she found me familiar, too.
But, she didn't. I found that out after crawling over a couple of people's
knees and staggering over to her side of the plane to say, "I noticed you
smiling at me. Do you know who I am?"

"No," she said, looking bewildered.

"Well, I know you," I said, surprising myself.

"Where in the world do you know me from?" she asked.

"Tell me," I began, "did you go to the Lebanon Country Club when you were a child?"

The Lebanon Country Club was a bungalow colony in Highland Mills, New York, one of hundreds of such colonies in the Catskill Mountains that was a popular place for predominantly urban Jews to go in the summer to escape the city heat.

"Yes," she said, her eyes widening.

"Is your name Leslie? Do you have a brother Ronnie?"

"Oh, my God," she replied. "You *do* know me!"

We chatted a little more and she gave me her contact information but then I had to sit down because the plane was doing a controlled crash landing into Fort Lauderdale and I was on my way to my beloved father's death bed. It was one day after my first book got published. My emotions were all over the place. In fact, I was beginning to believe that a crash landing would've been a poetic end to what was already a real roller coaster of a year.

My father did wait for me. We were able to spend some time together before he died in the wee hours of October 3rd.

I never did get in touch with Leslie because the following years were completely devoid of peace for me. But, a seed had been planted. The Lebanon Country Club brought back memories that may have remained buried had I not run into Leslie.

I believe I stayed at the Lebanon Country Club twice – once when I was six and once when I was eleven.

Bungalow colonies and kuchaleins (boarding houses where you cooked for yourself) were a tradition in my family. My grandparents had met at a kuchalein in the Catskills back in the 1920s. To my understanding, kuchaleins were the predecessors of bungalow colonies, where you also cooked for yourself but did so in the privacy of your own cottage. (Kuchalein literally means "cook alone.")

While fathers worked in the cruel heat of the city, mothers and children were deposited in boarding houses and, later, little cottages in the country for the summer. Fathers came up on weekends and got a little relief. The women entertained themselves with card games and clothing peddlers (also known as "blouse men") during the week and the children had day camp. Grandparents were always included in these summer getaways and grandmothers frequently wore halter tops that looked like brassieres long before Madonna. At least, that's how it was in the fifties, when I came along.

Before the Lebanon Country Club (aka Weg's), there was Saslow's and Woodbine and Orchard Mansion (aka Horseshit Mansion and Herbie's Paradise) which was in Moodus, Connecticut and a fabulous place aside from the bats. After Lebanon came Skopp's, where I met a girl who taught me how to smoke and kiss and bake brownies and dance Brooklyn-style. Nadine and I are still friends fifty years later.

We all had fun at these bungalow colonies – even after we moved from urban apartment buildings into relatively luxurious houses on Long Island with air conditioning and swimming pools. It was still great to go "to the country" and live in a cramped shack for a few weeks and fight mosquitos and skunks for the sheer joy of being among kindred spirits in play. Surely, these were days of heaven for me with a few strange, lingering recollections.

For example, I was already babysitting other people's children in bungalows by the time I was nine. That would be unheard-of today, but, back then, there was a couple that entrusted me with their three young children. One was an infant.

One night, they said, "A big thunderstorm is coming. Are you afraid of thunder?"

I said, "No."

Thunder I was okay with. It was the lightning that terrified me. And, Catskill thunderstorms were chock full of lightning. When the couple came home, I was huddled under their kitchen table with all three of their children.

Another time, I was being harassed by an older boy who wanted to break into the bungalow to steal liquor.

"I'll fix you a drink," I said, just to get rid of him. I made him a Bab-o cocktail that could've gotten rid of him permanently. Hey, I had babies to protect. Thank God, he threw up. Then he threatened to kill me for the rest of the summer. That was daunting. But, I was tough. It was my big brother who nearly got killed.

He made the mistake of calling some guy a pinhead. A really muscular guy. Turns out, the really muscular guy had a small head and had a thing about being called a pinhead. So, he punched my brother out.

"Get up and fight," I hissed at my brother.

"What, are you crazy?" he said from his prone position. "If I get up, he'll only knock me down again." So, I had a go at the big jock myself. Fortunately, I was friends with his sister (who protected me but also looked capable of knocking my brother down).

We shared a bungalow with another family when we were at the Lebanon Country Club in 1964. There were two separate units in one cottage but we were both across from a swamp that invited all sorts of flying insects into our living space. I was traumatized by moths and wasps going up in flames in the high intensity lamp in the kitchen. I still have nightmares about those self-immolating insects.

In the meantime, the little kid next door was a real nerd who was into chasing monarch butterflies with a net. His loutish father was always asking him, "You wanna potch?" (basically, a whack). My brother and I were always entertained by the constant litany of threats we heard through the wall that would've gotten the dumb shit thrown in jail today.

I also remember Color War, a week of athletic competition which included the writing of songs. My brother (who is now an entertainer) and I were both good at lyrics. I'm sure there were other contributors, as well. I remember one song that we wrote to the tune of "Sealed with a Kiss."

Here at Lebanon we're spending the summer
And, with every passing day
Our love forever grows
As we cherish the memories
Which in our hearts stay
We look up and see the blue sky above us
The warmth seems to burst from the sun
And, when the daylight ends
Then, the sky's kissed by moonlight
Another day is done

Nadine and I revised it the following year to, "Here at Skopp's Day Camp we're spending the summer." We recycled our lyrics. Why waste such beautiful words?

I recently found Lebanon Country Club camp pictures from 1964, buried in one of my memory boxes. There I am, standing in the back row with the counselors, along with the sister of the muscular pinhead. I was a tall girl. Seated in the lower right is Leslie – the woman from the plane.

We're all smiling. Life was good in the country.

PLEASE DON'T EAT ME

People have all sorts of ideas about how they want to be handled when they die. Some want to be buried, some cremated, etc. You know the options. A lot of the feelings surrounding how to dispose of yourself has to do with how you lived your life and how you related to others. I actually expect to live forever. Just not here.

THE BIG SENDOFF

SEPTEMBER 2015

I took care of my will a long time ago and, to me, the most difficult part was documenting how I wanted to be disposed of. I mean, it's not like you can change your mind posthumously.

I have one very religious friend who said, "Flush me down the toilet when I go because my body means nothing." If that's the truth, she's wasting a whole lot of money on cosmetic surgery. And, that's going to be one expensive plumbing job.

Sometimes I joke around about being put in an oregano jar and accidentally ending up on somebody's pizza, but it's really not a laughing matter. I'm sure that moldering in a grave isn't a barrel of laughs but at least you go in looking like yourself and not a pile of ashes. And then, there's that business of being locked into a vault in a mausoleum like you're some kind of savings bond. I mean, dead is dead, right? It's not like people are going to visit you in your old wedding dress – unless you're stuffed, and that doesn't seem right. They may visit your gravesite and think of you as you were. Or, have you in their thoughts wherever they are because sometimes you're nowhere and everywhere. As the song says, "All we are is dust in the wind."

When my twenty-one-year-old cat died some time back, I had already dug a hole for him in my backyard. But, I knew that at some point I would be moving from that place and I didn't want to abandon him in the cold ground. So, I trimmed some of his fur and had the rest of him cremated for portability purposes. Prior to the cremation, I took a ride with his body in a cardboard box and took him to all the places we loved being while he was alive. I admit, it was a rather morbid thing to do but I had to do it – for myself. I also did a ceremony for him at the ocean and watched the sea wipe his name from the sand. I took his cremains with me to Santa Fe.

If you're wondering what I did with his fur, I combined it with my hair and my husband's hair and placed it in a time capsule with pictures. I placed the time capsule in the hole that I dug in my backyard in Atlanta, near the woods where he used to play and hunt. Frankly, I buried a piece of all of us there.

People go out in all sorts of ways; some very quietly and some with a whole lot of fanfare. My father-in-law died one August and his cremains were laid to rest in an old family cemetery in North Florida. He had been cremated, not because he wanted to be but because he was practical and didn't want my mother-in-law to have to spend a whole lot of dough on disposing of him.

My father-in-law was a fifty-year Mason and had a Masonic sendoff. A bunch of guys in aprons and white gloves clapped hands and consigned Brother Zachary to Heaven while we all melted from the heat in our seats.

A few years later, Mama was also cremated (because her husband was) and buried in the same family plot. Lots of people showed up for her funeral because she was a well-known Southern historian and genealogist and a devout member of the Daughters of the Confederacy. She had wanted certain hymns sung at her funeral and two cousins came from Baxley, Georgia to oblige. One cousin sang while another played on a little synthesizer. Somewhere in the middle of the singing, I discovered that I was sinking into the sandy ground, along with every other woman who was there in high heels. The cousin playing the synthesizer was a very tall woman. By the time the singing ended, she probably topped out at five-foot-two. If it lasted any longer, we all would've been six feet under.

We ended the service with a rousing version of "Dixie" that we were sure Mama would've loved. A few of us were freaked out but, hey, it was her funeral. What she wouldn't have loved was what came next.

My brother-in-law had predeceased his mother by a couple of months. His girlfriend had brought his cremains to the cemetery so that he might be scattered on the family plot. I thought of it as a "Sack of Zach." (I should mention here that every male in my husband's family – except for my husband and his son – are named Zachary, and that was my brother-in-law's name as well as my father-in-law's name.) The girlfriend also brought some pickles, egg salad, a rose bush and a rather comatose sister.

The funeral director said to her in no uncertain terms, "You can't scatter ashes here. This is a cemetery!" That reminded me of a line out of "Dr. Strangelove," where one character says, "You can't fight in here. This is the war room!"

We had to wait until the ceremony was over and the crowd left before we figured out where to put Zach. He and his mother hadn't gotten along so we weren't going to throw him in the same hole (although the thought of them duking it out in perpetuity was almost too hard to resist). We ended up planting him near Daddy's grave, rose bush and all. In the meantime, my husband and I missed the sendoff party we had arranged at the house where Mama was raised. There was no food left by the time we got there – and we sure didn't want to eat the egg salad and pickles that had been left in the hot car all afternoon with the comatose sister while we tried to sneak Zach into the earth.

Most of the deceased members of my family are either in the ground or in a mausoleum. The Jewish elders, for the most part, wouldn't dream of cremation because they figured enough Jews were burned in Europe. The younger ones and those of different religious backgrounds seem to prefer cremation because they think it's quicker, cheaper and better for the environment. At least that sounds better than the reasoning of an acquaintance of my husband's from Minneapolis who had packages of his cremains shipped around to anyone he ever knew bearing the instruction, "Eat me."

My father had a sweet sendoff. Decades before, he had purchased an exquisite casket (my mother called it the Rolls Royce) and made arrangements for his interment in a beautifully-kept marble mausoleum where he anticipated being surrounded by his sisters and brothers-in-law. When the day came to check into his penthouse (his vault was on the very top floor – to be closer to Heaven, he had said), he looked so handsome and at peace. Both of his sisters and most of his brothers-in-law had predeceased him and he would, in fact, be surrounded by family for that big poker game in the sky. Unfortunately, my mother was at odds with one of his sisters (the one with the vault right next door) and was horrified at the prospect of lying beside her for all eternity.

I insisted upon throwing a party for my father following his burial so that friends and family could celebrate his life (and a few pool buddies could scarf down beer and pastrami sandwiches while trying to hit on my mother – but that's a whole other story).

Of course, my mother asked, "What does he need a party for?" Which brings me to this point: Once you're dead, it's all about the living and how they cope with your loss. I think that having people around who care for you (and the decedent, of course) is a very important part of the mourning process. And, if the spirit of the deceased is still present, they can enjoy one last romp with their loved ones before zipping off into the afterlife.

Who says that stardust can't have a little fun?

So, in my will, I have chosen not to document how I wish to be disposed of. I'm going to leave that decision to somebody else. I wouldn't mind the mausoleum route but the only mausoleum in Santa Fe faces a shopping center and only accepts Catholics. My parents' mausoleum is in a very beautiful cemetery but they don't accept non-Jews (that would leave my husband out) – and I don't want to be around my mother and aunt when they start brawling forever over stuff that didn't even matter when they were alive. And, I really don't want to end up on somebody's pizza.

There is a lovely memorial garden near where I used to live in Atlanta. People of all backgrounds are welcome. There's a pond and ducks and geese and I already know so many people who have a permanent home there. In fact, I still go there to chat with them.

I don't think anyone will ever come to visit me, though. I seem to be the one who does most of the visiting. But, it doesn't really matter, does it? There's something to be said for simply disappearing. It's how you're remembered that counts.

IT'S HERE

I enjoy the winter holidays. For me, they're one big party. A lot of people get stressed out, especially if they're going crazy over what to buy Aunt Buffy and Uncle George. I wasn't brought up around a whole lot of festivity and I don't think I received a wrapped present until I was an adult. But, the holiday season isn't about that for me. It's about expressing love in whatever form it takes. So – happy holidays to you all! I send you my love.

CHRISTMAS MEMORIES

DECEMBER 2015

A few years back, my husband came home from Starbuck's bearing a CD called, "Barbra Streisand: Christmas Memories." It kind of begged the question, "Is it a blank CD?" I mean, what kind of Christmas memories could Barbra Streisand have? I could understand, "Shavuot Memories." I could imagine "Pesach Memories." But, Barbra Streisand's "Christmas Memories"? Seriously? Maybe from watching "Miracle on 34th Street."

So, I looked at the CD to see if I recognized any songs (because I, like Barbra, have loads of Christmas memories).

I saw one: "I'll Be Home for Christmas." I don't think she was talking about her home in Flatbush. I never heard of the songs on the rest of the CD. They were, however, beautifully sung, with a cantorial sensibility.

I love Barbra Streisand. I think she is fabulously talented. But having Barbra put out a CD on her Christmas memories is like me putting out a book called, *I Remember Kwanzaa*. Get a grip, Yentl – you're Jewish.

I'm kidding, of course. We all have Christmas memories. How can we not? Christmas lights went up in August this year!

When I was a girl, Christmas was the time of year when many of my friends decorated trees and opened mountains of brightly-wrapped presents and actually anticipated Santa Claus coming down their chimneys, regardless of whether they were naughty or nice. They even put out a plate of cookies for old St. Nick and got up extra early on Christmas morning to see what he left for them. My husband tells me that his childhood Christmases were very magical.

We didn't have much festivity around Christmas time at my house. We did light a menorah, if my mother remembered to buy candles. We sang a little and, when my grandmother was around, we had delicious potato pancakes. The only gift we received was Chanukah gelt – which means money. When I was young, that meant three silver dollars. When I was a teenager, my father paid my brother and I off in cash for all the silver dollars we collected over the years and gave them to our cousins. Those rare silver dollars are now worth a fortune. The paper money equivalent was never worth a hill of beans. Oh, well.

I decorated my first Christmas tree when I worked at the Herricks Theater on Long Island as a sometimes cashier/sometimes popcorn girl. I was sixteen and it was mostly an X-rated theater (by today's standards, it would've been a PG-13). My boss was right off the boat from Ireland and quite stern. When she told me to card people twice, I carded people twice. When she told me to decorate the tree, I decorated the tree.

I didn't decorate it with matzo balls, either. It was the real McCoy – with strings of popcorn (that was easy enough, considering I was always up to my elbows in popcorn) and tinsel and assorted ornaments and rather large lights (not like the sleek lights of today). It was festive and I enjoyed it very much. Then I went home and fondled my gelt like Fagin. The silver dollars felt slippery and cold. And, they were handed out like lifesavers, not wrapped in pretty paper and tied in bows. Unless they were chocolate – in which case, they were individually wrapped in gold foil. Yummy money.

Chanukah was fine. I especially loved the singing. In fact, it was a real bonding experience for my father and me. In his later years, I called on holidays to sing with him over the phone – all the old songs that truly were my early holiday memories.

Before I met my husband, my ex and I used to enjoy spending Christmas at a friend's farm in Cumming, Georgia. If it wasn't cold enough for the cows' tongues to stick to the icy water in the trough, we would ride horses around the corral before dinner. Then, I met Grant, and we began celebrating Christmas with his parents in Linville Falls, North Carolina.

Christmas in the high country of Appalachia was magical, indeed. There was always a beautifully-decorated, hand-cut tree in the living room in front of the wood-burning fireplace (which was the only source of heat in the upper part of the house built by Grant's parents). There were always presents under the tree and heavy snow on the rhododendrons, Santa Claus plates and something delicious baking in the oven. One year, we gave

Mama and Daddy Bing Crosby's Christmas CD. They sat on the couch and held hands while we all listened to "White Christmas."

One of my sweetest memories of Christmas was taking our twenty-one-year-old cat on a ride around the Atlanta suburbs to see the lights. We even let him drive, while standing on Grant's lap. In one subdivision, we were all awed by the sight of a seven-point buck loping beside our car. It was our cat's final Christmas, and it couldn't have been a grander finale.

Grant and I now live in Santa Fe, New Mexico, where Christmas season means the Farolito Walk down Canyon Road on Christmas Eve (sometimes), the crisp air fragrant with the scent of burning pinion (always), trying to duplicate my grandmother's latkes, baking pecan puffs, the Desert Chorale and lots of partying with friends who have become our family here.

This year, we will celebrate with the family in Atlanta that hosted our wedding back in 1992. We went back to be with them a couple of years ago after they lost a son, who was our friend. It was a very joyous Christmas and we were very happy that we went because the father, also our friend, died suddenly before the next year was over. Part of the magic of the season for us is showing up – not because we're Santa Claus but because we love.

Every Christmas morning that we're home, Grant and I dance in the kitchen to Diana Krall's Christmas album. There are only three songs on it: "Have Yourself a Merry Little Christmas," "Christmas Time is Here" and "Jingle Bells." We will have already opened the presents that are placed around our fireplace, but not under a tree. I am always dressed in a white satin nightgown and Grant's father's Christmas tree socks. Grant is always barefoot and dressed in black drawstring pants.

We make our way around the appliances like Fred and Ginger, complete with twirls and dips, breathing a little more heavily each year. Now, we have a cat to watch us dance. I make banana walnut pancakes and hazelnut coffee. And, I think of harmonizing with my father, not only to "Rock of Ages" but also to "I'll Be Home for Christmas" because, like Barbra Streisand, we all have Christmas memories, no matter where we're coming from.

IT'S NOT ALL ABOUT FOOTBALL

Only three weeks, three days, three hours, three minutes and three seconds until Super Bowl Sunday. And counting. That's all I know about football. I wish I were a sports fan – at least it would provide a little fun distraction from everything else that's going on in the world. On the other hand, there's a lot of good stuff that goes on around football. And, that's what I wish for all of us this year. Good stuff.

GOOD STUFF

JANUARY 2016

Every year at this time, we start all over again. New taxes. New health insurance. New wrinkles. New resolutions, which I personally resolved decades ago not to make. Some of us have more eventful lives than others – marriages, divorces, travels, newborns, illnesses, encounters with terrorists. I don't know many people who have completely uneventful lives because they would be boring beyond belief (BBB).

We all want our lives to be filled with stuff. It's just better when our lives are filled with good stuff – but that means different things to different people. Everybody's good stuff is different. For example, a lot of people love to watch professional football. For me, it's BBB. When I told my former sister-in-law that I had no interest in watching football, she told me to get a life. I told her I had one, which is why I didn't watch football. She didn't get it. Why? Because, for her, watching football was good stuff. Okay – so call me a freak of nature. I wasn't born with the sports fan gene.

However, there was a time in my life when I watched football games and loved the experience. I had a boyfriend who was a huge New England Patriots fan and I was a huge fan of my boyfriend so when he wanted to take me to football games in Foxboro, Massachusetts on snowy Sunday afternoons, I gladly went. I especially enjoyed the tailgate parties, where I felt like I was living in a Lowenbrau commercial: tall, athletic men; friendly, hardy women; brats steamed in beer and vats of seafood chowder.

Once the game started, I wanted to dive into the chowder because I was cold beyond belief (CBB). There's something about sitting in stands on a snowy day watching what looked like forty-cubic-foot refrigerators in helmets bashing into each other for hours that made me feel like I was going to freeze to death. I used to beg extra clothing from strangers but I could have been wearing a fur-lined bison and still frozen my ass off. My boyfriend tried pouring the contents of his flask down my throat. I couldn't hold the flask myself with frozen fingers and twelve pairs of gloves. I didn't realize that the brandy was lowering my already arctic body temperature but at least it made me too drunk to care.

It wasn't like I wasn't wearing every article of clothing I owned. I looked like the Michelin Man. But it was never enough. I still suffer from the cold.

So, I sat in the stands with my teeth chattering and asked brilliant questions like, "What just happened?" My boyfriend made patient attempts to edify me while he screamed his head off with the rest of the crowd. Boston sports fans are an excitable group.

There was one goofy-looking guy who showed up for every game. He sat a few rows down from us and didn't have a tooth in his head. I'll bet he lost those choppers at a football game. At any rate, every time the Patriots scored, he would turn to face the crowd with arms outstretched and yell, "I love them." Without teeth, it sounded like "I wub dem." And, the crowd always shouted back, "Shut the fuck up!" Wow – they were even tough to their own kind.

I always felt like getting up and dancing around with the cheerleaders at halftime, just to get some circulation back in my legs but my gams were so stiff I would be dancing like Peter Boyle putting on the Ritz in "Young Frankenstein." Not to mention it would be hard to do a split wearing a fur-lined bison.

At any rate, after the game, I would return all borrowed clothing and my boyfriend would carry my ossified body back to the car and start the defrosting process. It was like I was a one hundred and twenty-pound turkey. And, speaking of turkey, all of that coldness made me feel like I had mainlined a gallon of tryptophan. We tried playing *Clue* once after a game and I fell asleep on Colonel Mustard.

So, let me remember what I loved about football. The boyfriend. The tailgate party. Beer-steamed brats. Hot chowder. The good men and women I met. Halftime. The toothless doofus. Brandy. And finally, Colonel Mustard. I guess I still found the game itself BBB. Oh, well. That's my quirk.

Do I go to Super Bowl parties? You bet I do! I may not know who's playing but I still enjoy socializing while listening to people scream at the TV. Speaking of Super Bowl Sunday, my husband and I once took a walk in the Georgia woods on that day and were stupid enough to ask another couple of hikers (or maybe they were just a couple of mean-looking guys with banjos) who was playing. They looked at us like we had antennae growing out of our heads. We didn't ask them twice. In fact, we became a pretty good pair of running backs that day.

So, where was I? This was supposed to be a story about the new year and good stuff.

What will your good stuff be this year? I would like to publish another book. I would like to create art for book covers. I would like my drawings to appear in The New Yorker. I would like to spend more time with people I care for. I would like to hike in the woods with my husband and not ask any more stupid questions. I would like to be able to see clearly. And, I would like to dance like a cheerleader at halftime. Now, *that* wouldn't be BBB. At least, not for me.

NOT HIGH ON COCAINE

When it comes to public transportation, I'd probably be better off if I were high on something. Because I'm a bit of a control freak and I like to determine when I come and when I go. You don't have that freedom when someone else is in charge of the ride. But, alas, I am not a recreational drug user, so I must suck it up and accept that, sometimes, you've just got to leave the driving to somebody else. As the Grateful Dead said, "Casey Jones you better, watch your speed."

RIDING THAT TRAIN

MARCH 2016

I grew up in a one-car family. My mother never learned how to drive, rendering life safer for all humanity in the western hemisphere. But, it also meant that, while my father was at work, the rest of us walked everywhere because the words, "public transportation," were unheard of in our house. And, that was a bit of problem because when you live on Long Island, you pretty much need a car to get around. My brother and I may have bummed a ride or two and we did have bicycles – but more than anything, we used our own two feet.

I think my mother always walked, even when she lived in the Bronx, which is why she's probably in such good shape at ninety. I'm having trouble imagining her in a subway car. And, I'm sure she never took a cab anywhere. So, her life was pretty much limited to where her feet could bring her, until my father got home.

After my father died, my mother continued to do all that she could to avoid the dreaded public transportation. When she needed to go shopping, she began to rely upon the services of a married man who was sweet on her. "Mom," I said, "I don't want to think about you prostituting yourself for a lift." It was time to move her to an independent living facility – and she gladly went for the free rides, even if she had to share them with other residents.

Getting back to my youth. I don't know why my mother was so freaked out by public transportation. Maybe she was afraid of getting lost or maybe it was the loss of control. Once you enter the world of public transportation, you're really at someone else's mercy. You've got to come and go when they say so and, if you take the wrong bus or train, you may end up in Iceland (or Islip). So, my brother and I were raised with an inherent lack of trust in – well, everything.

My father, who frequently used public transportation, like the Long Island Railroad and the New York subway system, reinforced this fretfulness. For example, when I was fifteen, I was on a date with my college-aged boyfriend in Manhattan. We were supposed to meet my father at a certain time and were en route to doing just that when my father caught sight of me on a bus. When I tell you he went absolutely berserk on 34th Street and started leaping around shouting my name and flailing his arms, it created a panic in me so intense I could have jumped out of the nearest closed bus window. What I did instead was start yelling, "Stop the bus! Stop the bus!" I didn't even know about the pull cord. I was going to get off at the next stop anyway and meet my father like a normal person. There was nothing normal about the hysteria that was foisted upon me. Needless to say, the boyfriend was history. And, I didn't get on a bus again for years after that.

My father sometimes got nervous, even when he was in charge of his own vehicle. One day, he accidentally went the wrong way on a one-way street in Atlanta. In a tizzy, he found a policeman and asked, "What should I do? What should I do?" The cop calmly said, "Turn around."

The first time I got on an airplane, it was also my mother's first time. As the plane lifted off from JFK, my mother was clearly terrified and made no secret of it. She nearly tore my arm off and suggested we were going to crash any minute – which has an impact on a twelve-year-old. There was actually nothing wrong with the flight. I have taken many flights since then that have been seriously terrifying – bad turbulence with flight attendants falling all over themselves, flying sideways with people praying on all sides, landing hard with passengers yelling "Shit!" in six different languages (I counted), stalling in violent crosswinds – you get the picture. You've probably been on a few of those flights yourself. So, what's the big deal? We've all lived to tell the story.

I know it's more dangerous to drive in your own personal vehicle than take a public conveyance (unless you're in a cab in New York City with a deranged driver from Eastern Europe with a death wish). But it's nice to be able to come and go as you please without standing around in the dark waiting for a stranger (or a vehicle filled with strangers) to pick you up.

Still, if you want to live in this world, sometimes you have to turn over the wheel to somebody else and have some faith that they will get you where you need to go without mishap.

But sometimes, there is a mishap. Like when my husband and I got on a glass-bottomed tourist boat in Key West. I have issues with motion sickness on boats in general but I had previously taken cruises without feeling like jumping overboard so how bad could this be?

Well, let me tell you. Before we took off for what was to be a two-hour cruise, the captain made an announcement on the PA. "We have ten-foot seas today, ladies and gentlemen. So, if you have trouble with motion sickness, you may want to get off the boat." I should have heeded his advice. Everybody should have heeded his advice because seconds after we set sail, everybody except my husband and the captain were on their hands and knees, hurling copiously.

I was laid out on a bench, waiting for the kind release of death, when I heard the captain's voice again. He said, "Well, ladies and gentlemen – for those of you who are still on your feet – here comes a school of yellowfin tuna." All I heard was "Blurgh" from all sides and my own laugh eerily bubbling up through my misery. Then, the captain added, "Of course, you can't really see the yellowfin tuna because we're in ten-foot seas and the sand is really agitated." Yeah – like the sand was the only thing that was agitated.

It was a terrible experience – one that stayed with me for days – but I did get to make a public service announcement after we got back to shore. I told the people on line to look at my yellow face and figure out if they wanted to get on the boat. They all fled like I had turned into Godzilla.

Okay, so I was a victim of my own stupidity. It wouldn't be the last time. A few years ago, my friend, Jeff, talked me into taking a kayak ride on the Weeki Wachee River, which is the maritime equivalent of Grand Central Station during rush hour. I hadn't kayaked in a long while so Jeff kindly tethered my kayak to his kayak. You might say I turned over the reins of my vehicle. But, this was no gentle drift down the Nile. There was, as mentioned, a whole lot of traffic on the Weeki Wachee that day and I accidentally ended up in a copse of trees which flipped my kayak. As I sunk into the river, amid the water snakes and alligators and manatees, I looked up and all I could see were the bottoms of boats. I contemplated the likelihood of drowning until I saw an opening and zoomed up to be rescued. So much for relinquishing control. On the other hand, if I were manning my own kayak, I would've ended up in the drink anyway – I simply wasn't any good at it.

Getting back to public transportation, another thing that gets to me is the inescapable exposure to people who sound like they belong in a tuberculosis ward. Sick people should stay home. And some physically healthy people should also avoid public encounters entirely like my friend, Jean, who wears a mask in airplanes for her own protection. Nobody will sit next to her, including her own husband. Even if the plane is completely full. Travelers will take another flight altogether to avoid flying with Jean. People are edgy enough these days about flying without having to deal with a nervous person in a mask.

I have been stuck in flooded train tunnels. I've been on cog trains and cable cars and narrow gauge railroads and tiny planes and big ships and speed boats and rental car transports and pickups driven fast over rutted roads. I've been on buses driven by yodeling drivers. I've traveled with enthusiastic people and nauseas people. I've hitched rides with strangers who wanted to end it all. I've been felt up at airports by TSA agents who seemed to enjoy that part of their job too much. I've sat next to nervous people on planes who have held my hand for reassurance. I probably would have made out with them if the plane were actually in danger of going down. Even if they had a cold.

So, what am I getting at? I think that public transportation is great if you're trying to be energy-efficient, want to get high and leave the driving to someone else, want to save a few bucks on gas or if you don't mind waking up next to a wino in Coney Island when you wanted to get off on Wall Street. Other than that, I find train travel romantic. I actually do like buses with great, big windows. And, nothing beats air travel for getting from one place to another relatively quickly (and I say "relatively" because when you fly from Albuquerque, it can take you thirty-seven years to get to Europe. With stops. And, if you're lucky, not in the middle of the Atlanta Ocean. You could probably walk to Europe faster.)

Which brings me back to my mother. I'm very happy that she's still walking and getting the occasional ride without putting out. As for my father, I wish he were still here to keep me on my toes every time I venture out of his comfort zone. My parents created a bit of a fretful control freak in me but I'm happy to say that I still get around. I haven't lost any other boyfriends due to freaking out on a bus. And, I can honestly say I haven't ever gotten lost on public transportation, although my husband nearly ended up in Warsaw after boarding a train to Amsterdam on a business trip. But he doesn't let these little screw-ups bother him. That's why he looks fifty and I look ninety – unlike my mother, who looks seventy-five.

I think I'm going to take a nice, soothing gondola ride and chill out. As long as I can do my own singing.

.

HOT STUFF

I have way too much electricity in my body and that's a drag because it seems like every time I touch something, I, or somebody else, get fried. I know that most people get zapped when they walk on carpet and then touch something metallic. I, on the other hand, could be standing on cement and will still practically incinerate the poor cat when I touch him. Seriously, I feel like the character, Jubilee, from the X-Men series: the one who is capable of creating pyro-kinetic sparks from her hands. Guess I'd better keep my hands to myself! And, forget about becoming a massage therapist!

WE WILL WE WILL SHOCK YOU

JUNE 2016

I don't know what the deal is with me, but there's a good reason I look like Roseanne Roseannadanna. I'm electrified, and, by that, I don't mean thrilled or captivated (I looked up "electrified" in the dictionary – it *does* mean thrilled or captivated but it also means electrically charged. That's me.)

I've had a lot of strange experiences with electricity in my life and it makes me wonder where I'm coming from. I mean, one time, I nearly electrocuted a horse. Of course, that had something to do with trying to touch him over an electrified fence (I got thrown a few feet myself, much to my husband's amusement). But, even without the electrified fence, I'm dangerous.

Take, for example, the time I knocked a young massage therapist across the room just for rubbing my forearm. I didn't actually haul off and hit him (after all, he was only rubbing my forearm). It was the flame that shot out of my arm with explosive force that did it. Hey – I damn near fell off the massage table, myself.

Now, every time I get a massage, I have to warn the therapist about the electricity in my body – especially in my left forearm. If they rub me the wrong way, there won't be a happy ending. Just an ending. Possibly a fatal ending.

My own husband is a little afraid to kiss me. He kind of has to extend a finger and touch me on the shoulder first (notice how I said shoulder and not forearm). Only then does he feel safe to approach my lips with his. It's an important precaution. You really don't want to have someone yelling "Goddamnit" and setting your nose on fire every time they kiss you. It's a buzz kill. On the other hand, once it's safe to proceed, he really does get a big charge out of kissing me. We not only have chemistry. We have electricity.

Unfortunately, I do end up yelling, "Goddamnit" every time I flip a light switch or touch the refrigerator or a car door handle. It's not like I'm picking up static from carpets. I'm walking on travertine, but the cat's fur still stands up when he sees me coming because he knows that Mommy is going to shock him. Poor Sparky. (Okay, you caught me. Everybody knows that my cat's name is Alfie.)

For some reason, I have always been afraid of lightning because I seem to attract it. I was once on the phone with a tenant who was hysterical because a mudslide had just come cascading through her living room. As I was contemplating how I could help her, the tree outside my window got stricken by lightning. It literally exploded, frying every appliance in the house with a motherboard. It could've happened to anyone in the neighborhood. After all, it was Atlanta in the summer and Atlanta's like one big lightning storm in the summer. But, it happened to me. At least the house didn't burn down. Perhaps I am a human lightning rod.

Sometimes, I'm just present when someone else is getting electrocuted. No, I'm not talking about an execution. When my ex-husband and I were sailing around the Aegean on our honeymoon, we had a bathroom in our stateroom that was an accident waiting to happen. There was a drain in the middle of the room and an overhead shower. When you took a shower, the whole room got soaked.

Well, one day, my ex took a shower and the drain wasn't working properly. He ended up standing in water up to his ankles. That's when he decided to plug in his electric razor. I suddenly heard a great, loud explosion and he went flying sideways out of the bathroom and nearly crashed through the porthole. This may make me sound a little sadistic but it had to be one of the funniest things I ever saw in my entire life (aside from the time my current husband nearly got sexually violated by a rutting elk that he was trying to photograph in Banff. But, that's a whole other story.)

I now live in Santa Fe, New Mexico where you can see storms coming from a hundred miles away in every direction. There are no trees around to obstruct your view. My husband loves the storms. He calmly watches them while I run around like Edith Bunker, trying to find shelter in our house, which is made almost entirely of glass.

Just before we moved here, around eleven years ago, we were visiting Santa Fe when an amazing storm came. By amazing, I mean it looked like *War of the Worlds*. I literally felt like we were in a bowl of fire. We went up to a place called Museum Hill and I just stood there screaming because I couldn't imagine a creature left alive or a house left standing anywhere in town. It was that intense. And, with all that lightning, not a drop of rain!

When we managed to survive this apocalypse, I called our realtor, who had lived in Santa Fe for over a decade, and asked her if the previous night's storm was anything unusual. She said, "Are you kidding? I was SCREAMING!" There we were – two middle-aged women from Long Island screaming in the Southwestern desert over a lightning storm.

I wish I had a picture of that. Taken with a flash.

SLOWLY I TURNED...

You gotta love technology. On a recent road trip, Siri very capably steered my husband, Grant, and I all over the Northeast. She even corrected us when we veered off course. Grant was impressed because he's a great orienteer and can find his way around the moon without assistance – but, even he had to admit that Siri was very good. The other technology that helped me on this trip was text messaging, most notably with my friend, Carl, who we were meeting up with in Niagara Falls, along with his wife, Starr. When Grant and I got stuck in traffic twelve feet away from the Canadian border for hours, it was texting with Carl that kept me from giving Abbott and Costello and The Three Stooges a run for their money. Because without his company, I would've gone truly berserk.

NIAGARA FALLS!

OCTOBER 2016

I'm a pretty patient person, usually, unless I'm surrounded by idiots and then all patience goes right out the window.

It all started when my dear friend and former business associate, Carl, invited my husband, Grant, and I to go on a short road trip with him and his wife, Starr. Originally, the trip was going to begin in Cleveland, which is where Carl and his wife now live, but my husband and I had to be in New England so we decided to take individual road trips that would lead us to one another. That's when we came up with Niagara Falls as a reasonable meeting point, on the Canadian side.

Of course, whenever I hear the words, "Niagara Falls," I have to break into that old "Slowly I Turned" routine made popular by both Abbott and Costello and The Three Stooges. You know the story: Some guy has his heart broken by his wife who runs off with another guy in, you guessed it, Niagara Falls. So, every time he hears the words, "Niagara Falls," he goes berserk and tries to kill the poor bastard who has innocently uttered them. Or maybe you don't know the story. Carl and Starr didn't, so they didn't understand why I kept yelling, "Niagara Falls! Slowly I turned, step by step, inch by inch," before grabbing my husband by the neck and attempting to strangle him to death. They just figured it was one of my antics.

Actually, I attempted to strangle Grant several times on the way to you-know-where, just for fun. But it's not generally a good idea to strangle someone while they're driving. Just saying.

To get to Niagara Falls (!), we had to drive from Stockbridge, Massachusetts, which is a nice six-hour trip across the Berkshires and upper New York State on the Mass Pike. It was a delightful fall day, with great patches of autumn color and occasional downpours, but we enjoyed every bit of the journey.

At the same time we were approaching from the east, Carl and Starr were approaching from the west. Carl and I thought it would seem more like a shared road trip if we exchanged texts along the way. It went like this:

Mindy: Is it raining where you are?

Carl: No, very sunny.

Mindy: Raining here but not much traffic. Will be on the cool side tomorrow.

Carl: LOL - I'm wearing shorts.

Mindy: I'm dressed like Nanook of the North.

Carl: (Laughing with tears emoji)

Mindy: We're about a hundred miles outside of Buffalo. ETA to hotel around 5:05 pm. Hope none of us get hung up at the border. I may get detained for my outfit alone. I don't know how Canadians feel about neon Spandex.

Carl: No problem. We'll meet in prison (smiley emoji). We're at the border. We'll ask about Spandex and let you know. LOL

Mindy: LOL...We'll be there ourselves within the hour.

Carl: (Cool emoji with sunglasses) Found out. No problem with Spandex. But they don't allow neon. Confirmed that you get one call. You have my number.

Mindy: Help! I need some subdued spray paint!

Carl: (Sends me a picture of the "neon lane" at Customs)

Mindy: (Emoji sticking out green tongue) The GPS just informed us we've been diverted to the Mexican border. We still have a ways to go. Would you please check on some possible dining options? I'm guessing seven would be a good time. We eat everything except Canadian food. And Mexican.

Carl: We just checked in. There are several restaurants around the area so there shouldn't be a problem finding a place to eat. The hotel recommended a steak place next door, but we're very flexible as long as the restaurant has a good bar.

We were both having a great chuckle until Grant and I finally approached the Rainbow Bridge, which takes you from the seedy New York side of Niagara Falls to the Reno-esque Canadian side of Niagara Falls. Ah – so near and, yet, so far. That was when I really began to feel like strangling people. And, here's the reason why.

Mindy: We're stacked up in front of the Rainbow Bridge. Latest ETA is 5:25. Is the hotel okay? I'm afraid we may be backed up until Monday morning. Not budging. I'm going to get up on the car roof and twerk. Everyone will run to South Dakota.

Carl: We can see the Rainbow Bridge from our window, so please don't twerk. (Emoji with hands extended - like "Gentlemen, I implore you.") "The hotel is about what you would expect. Don't worry about the time. We're going to find a bar. Just text us when you're ready to meet up.

Mindy: Did you also come across the Rainbow Bridge?

Carl: No, the Peace Bridge.

Mindy: That explains it. We're still sitting here – very slowly approaching the Un-Peaceful Bridge. Haven't been through Customs. The ETA now shows 7:14. I'm not sure if that's a.m. or p.m. Do you think the bar delivers? After we locate the hotel, we'll check in and need to freshen up. Will text you ASAP.

Carl: K. Thx. Sorry. (Sad emoji).

Mindy: I'm looking for a hara-kiri emoji. (Laughing with tears emoji).

Carl (Dark emoji) Will this work? Where are you? On the bridge yet?

Mindy: LOL...Just got on the bridge but barely moving. It's unreal. I'll have a double. If you can still see the bridge, I'll flash my neon at you! Maybe I'll blind the other drivers. Looks like we're going to have to pee in the Niagara River.

Carl: I've heard the expression "Cry Me a River," but...(smiley emoji, hands extended).

Mindy: I'm looking for a barrel right now. I've been behind some idiot from New Jersey for the past five-hundred hours. It's a good thing our windows are closed 'cuz I'm sounding a little like Tony Soprano. And, don't get me started on the fat-assed morons on very loud motorcycles revving their engines on one side of us and the doofus on the other side who's smoking himself to death. Of course, they're electronic cigarettes. He's competing with the falls to make mist. Arrgghhh! Where's the arsenic when you need it? And, the GPS is now giving me an ETA of the twelfth of never.

And, then...

Mindy: Approaching Customs. Eventually. I've grown a long beard and bushy eyebrows. Just like the picture on my passport.

Carl: Great! Just found out this weekend is Canadian Thanksgiving – second Monday in October. BTW, they have restrooms here.

All I can say is thank God for texting and Carl's sense of humor. I was actually having quite a meltdown in the car. My calm and sensible husband was merely dismayed, like a normal person. Turns out, it wasn't only Canadian Thanksgiving weekend. It was also Columbus Day weekend in the States. Apparently, people were dying to get out of the U.S. (I can just imagine the length of the line leaving the States if Mr. Pussy wins the election!)

So, we did manage to meet up for dinner minutes after we made it to our hotel. I got out of my neon Spandex and changed into something less comfortable while Grant parked our rental car. Over the next thirty-six hours, the four of us had a fabulous time doing the things that people do in Niagara Falls. And, when the weekend was over, we knew we wanted to make these road trips a tradition. We already missed Carl and Starr before we breezed back over the Rainbow Bridge on Canadian Thanksgiving/Columbus Day morning.

So, I sent Carl a text.

Mindy: Where shall we rendezvous next?

Carl: Maybe we can meet in Napa!?

Mindy: I'll prepare my robe.

Carl didn't respond to that and I didn't understand why until I checked on my messages a week later. That's when I felt like an idiot. So, I sent him another text.

Mindy: Oh! I thought you wrote Nepal (chagrined emoji). Napa would be great! And, no robes required!

PARTYING IN SANTA FE

Santa Fe is Party Central, especially during holiday season. But, if you're looking for people dressed in slinky cocktail dresses and fancy suits at corporate holiday parties, you've come to the wrong place. This is not a town with corporations. It's artsy-Western-chic. You dress in cowboy dusters and turquoise jewelry and maybe spurs, if your horse has been invited, when you go to parties around here and most of the better parties take place in private homes with amazing buffets and fabulous artwork and water features that run even when it's freezing out. On the other hand, if you choose to wear spike heels and an eighty-year-old cashmere sweater, nobody will tell you not to.

A TALE OF TWO SWEATERS

DECEMBER 2016

It's holiday season once again and my husband and I are forming a tradition with a pair of friends to get dressed to the nines and crash parties at hotels and casinos in Santa Fe and Albuquerque. Okay, maybe "crash" is too strong a word. We're not actually sneaking in to corporate parties and hobnobbing with strangers over pate and trying to get them to believe that we work offsite and that's why nobody knows who the hell we are. It's more like we observe people who actually know each other attending these parties. Hmmm. Sounds a little like stalking. Anyway, we did it at a casino in Albuquerque last year and our friends regretted that we weren't decked out like the partygoers. So, this year, we decided to dress up and go to a fancy restaurant in a posh hotel in Santa Fe and watch strangers partying before and after dinner in an environment that's closer to home.

Funny thing is, there aren't a whole lot of corporations in Santa Fe and when people get together, it's normally at other people's houses or at intimate bars where everybody knows your name and knows who you are and knows whether you belong at that particular party or not.

Having lived in Santa Fe for more than twelve years where dressing up means wearing your un-scuffed cowboy boots and clean jeans, it had been a while since I had to get duded up here. Typically, you don't wear high heels in Santa Fe (unless you're a hooker) because you either tear them up or fall down and kill yourself on gravel driveways. But this was going to be an elevator ride from a parking garage to a lobby so I felt confident I wouldn't take a dive into the arms of a partying stranger.

I do have a closet full of old party dresses and suits from my corporate days. Finding one that was appropriate posed a little bit of a challenge. The suits were mostly unwearable because they all have 1980's-style football shoulders. And some of the dresses didn't fit quite right or had to be worn without bras, which didn't seem right. I also needed to find out if my old nylon stockings had turned to cheese. I bought a pair just in case, but I was able to return them because the nylons had held up better than I had.

Of course, what I chose was sleeveless and I get cold easily so I had to come up with something warm and attractive to go with it. I wouldn't be caught dead in my mother's mink stole (even though the mink had been dead for ages) because it just screamed ANIMAL KILLER. I needed something a little subtler – something that looked like faux fur because who would trim a sweater with real fur these days?

I have two sweaters that I inherited from my paternal grandmother, who was a very beautiful and elegant woman from the Old Country. Nana Bertha was an amazing seamstress and made some of her own beautiful clothing out of garments she purchased and then ripped apart and reconstructed to suit herself. These sweaters are made out of one hundred percent imported cashmere, lace, diamonds (real ones, I suspect), pearls (ditto) and, you guessed it, mink. The real stuff – but only around the collar and down the front. To tell you the truth, it's surprising that these sweaters have not been eaten by moths over the years. And, they have been around, in a variety of closets in a variety of states, for over eighty years!

So, our friends and we came up the hotel elevator expecting to run into a party that would equal one thrown by the Great Gatsby himself and...there was nobody there! And, by nobody, I mean absolutely nobody. So, we sashayed our fancy selves down to the bar, where we initially sat in very pretty but dysfunctional seats that made the men look like midgets. That didn't seem right so we switched over to a table in front of a roaring fire. Hey, there was nobody there - we could have sat in the fire and nobody would've noticed. The fire was so big I'm surprised my husband's tie didn't burst into flames. I, of course, had to take off my stunning sweater because it was too damn hot in there. I think the heat actually melted my friend's stockings.

We finally got up and entered the nearly-empty, but still-lovely, dining room. We gave our order and got served around two hours later. If the place was busy, we'd probably still be sitting there now, getting soused. We were going to have a nightcap afterward but decided to move the party to where we might be able to actually party. So, we drove off to a local piano bar, where we know the piano player, and lo and behold – one of those private parties was about to begin and, because we live in a small town, the proprietor knew we didn't belong there. Even the piano player wasn't invited to this one. It was for film festival people. Not outsiders, like us.

So, we drove off once again, this time to a place that features jazz and tapas. And, we did get noticed a little. Some guy who looked like he was a member of the Lithuanian mafia grabbed my husband by the arm and said, "Nice tie, man." Outside of a bolo, nobody in this town has seen a tie in – well, ever. I did catch a couple of people eyeballing the fur on my sweater, like I murdered someone's house cat. (As a matter of fact, it looks so much like a cat that when I went to put it on, I discovered our cat trying to mate with it on the guest bed.) There were a lot of people at the jazz and tapas bar but nobody was in fancy evening attire, so we had nobody to gawk at (all right, I may have gawked at the Lithuanian mafia guy a little but only because he looked dangerous).

I'll tell you one thing. I was very happy to have my nana's sweater when I left that place because nighttime in Santa Fe in December is cold. In fact, I wish I had the other sweater, too. Maybe I'll wear both next time – with my mother's stole on top. And, maybe a dead house cat. In Albuquerque.

BRING GODZILLA ON

You can look at Godzilla in two different ways. He can either scare the bejesus out of you because, one, he's a big, scary reptile that incinerates people and two, he doesn't care who he incinerates; or, he can make you laugh because one, he looks ridiculous even when he's incinerating people, and two, you do know he's not real, right?

OUT OF CONTROL

MAY 2017

I think I've always been a little over the top when it comes to controlling myself in public. I mean, it's not every high school girl who gets her whole class thrown out of Philharmonic Hall by laughing hysterically at a Shostakovich piece because it sounds like background music for a Godzilla movie. I tried to control myself, but I could truly envision some fire-spewing monstrosity incinerating concert-goers as he plodded down the center aisle of the theater to the dramatic cacophony of Symphony No. 5.

It started with a slight grimace. Then, as I tried to suppress my laughter, I began to shake. Then, the whole row began to shake. Then, the teacher, Mr. Carbone, began to shake. Boy, was he disappointed in me – he had never gotten heave-hoed out of the Philharmonic before. But he was cracking up while he dressed me down. I mean, especially when I told him about the Godzilla part. That got me off lightly with Mr. Carbone, who was a real sweetie, anyway.

Years earlier, I had gotten my whole family evicted from a religious service because a rabbi with a pompous Hungarian accent was pontificating about some Old Testament guy who tied his ass to a tree and walked for forty miles in the desert. Well, number one, how do you walk with your ass tied to a tree? And, number two, how do you find a tree in the desert to tie your ass to? These were the questions that I was pondering when I burst into uncontrollable laughter. My brother and mother certainly couldn't control themselves, so we were all thrown out on *our* asses. And, we were sitting in the front row, no less. My father sat sadly shaking his head In the choir loft. Man, was he embarrassed.

But, he was a little out of control himself. Like the time he brought me up to a Borscht Belt hotel for a summer job interview. I was applying for a cocktail waitressing position and was meeting with a guy named Chernoff. Unfortunately, I was a little nervous and kept calling him Mr. Jerkoff. My father had to be scraped off the carpet over that one. And, no, I didn't get the job. Hey – I was being polite. I did say Mister.

Life is a great, big tragedy a lot of the time – especially these days, when we're probably on the verge of extinction. But sometimes, things just strike me as insanely funny. People say and do ridiculous things and they are completely innocent about it. Like when my mother described a play about a fat man as a good, meaty story. Like when my in-laws gave detailed instructions on how to grow taters. Like when I hastily poured my sister-in-law a glass of wine out of a carafe at a winery in North Georgia and she really enjoyed it – until the sommelier informed her that she just drank from the swill bucket. Like when a hiking companion in New Mexico started throwing stones at a bull on a trail to get him to move and I was standing there in a red sweatshirt feeling like a picador without a lance. I mean, you think about something like that afterward and you just lose it. At least, I do.

I asked the stone thrower's wife, "What do we do if the bull charges us?"

"Jump into a tree," she said.

Yeah, like there are trees in New Mexico's high desert. Actually, there was one small tree. I could have tied my ass to it and maybe the bull would've impaled me as I attempted to trudge across the wasteland for forty miles. Too bad we didn't have any rope.

I like to laugh and I like to make people laugh. I don't even care what I look like, anymore. Hey, I figure if I can't look good, I may as well look ridiculous. I don't think there's anything more to say about that.

I CAN'T MAKE THIS STUFF UP

I haven't found much to laugh about lately but I'm happy to say I recall the last time I laughed my head off and it was with my father, over the most inane of experiences. We were laughing at the expense of others, but only because they had completely laughable names. One or two may have escaped our notice, but a whole neighborhood filled with goofy-named people was too much for us to handle without losing it. I am so glad we had that last laugh together. And, I wonder if I'll ever laugh like that again.

THE LAST LAUGH

OCTOBER 2017

Back in 2003, my husband, Grant, and I picked up a small piece of investment property on the coast of Georgia in a new development built around a Fred Couples golf course. It seemed like a good idea at the time. The environment was going to be kept as natural as possible, complete with jaguars and alligators and beautiful live oaks dangling Spanish moss. There was going to be a nice club house and a high-water marina on St. Andrew's Sound and it just seemed too good to pass up. So, we became proud owners of swampland in Georgia. And, so did many other people. The properties sold out in no-time-flat. While we didn't expect to live there anytime soon, we were pleased with our investment.

We moved from Atlanta to Santa Fe, New Mexico in 2005 and, while we paid our taxes and association fees and utility bills for our property in Georgia, we didn't get to see the property much. Then, all of a sudden in 2007, we had a perfect opportunity to visit our little piece of heaven with my parents in tow.

My father had heard from an old college roommate from the University of Montana, who was now living in a senior facility in Jacksonville. The roommate, Dawson, managed to track my father down in Delray Beach via the Internet and really wanted to see him again. It had been sixty-five years, after all. Nobody was getting any younger.

At first, my father, who was in his early eighties, balked. He hadn't driven on a highway in years and was nervous about it. I had heard about Dawson my whole life (he was a successful reporter) and I wanted to meet him before he wasn't around anymore (he was older than my father and not as fit). So, I made a deal with my father. If he and my mother made the four-hour trip up to Jacksonville to stay with Dawson and his girlfriend, Pearl, Grant and I would fly to Jacksonville from Albuquerque, hang out with everyone and then take my parents on a ride up to Waverly, Georgia so they could see our property.

This all sounded like a little too much adventure for my parents but I convinced my father that the sin of omission was worse than the sin of commission. So, it was decided: We were all going to have an adventure.

We all met up in Jacksonville and had a nice visit with Dawson and Pearl. My father was happy that he took to the highway. He was now looking forward to the Georgia adventure.

The day we headed up to our property was a bright and beautiful day in early December. We got to the subdivision and everything looked perfect. No high-water marina yet (or, possibly, ever) but the golf course looked great and the properties were well maintained and we were all having a good time.

Each piece of property had the names of the owners on a stake at the curb, including ours. Very nice signs. Ours said, "The Hollands, Santa Fe, NM" and our two-tenths of an acre was lush with subtropical growth. We were well located between the marsh and the golf club on a very civilized-looking street.

My usually-cynical father was very impressed with what he saw. He even said, more than once, that he thought we made a very good investment. Plus, he was a former golfer and he knew a good golf course when he saw one.

We parked the car in front of our property and got out to explore our cul-de-sac. My mother, who has the world's best vision, suddenly pointed a finger and said, "Look – You live next door to the Gays." I kidded, "Well, that's nice. It wouldn't be for the first time." That's when she noticed the neighbors on the other side. They were the Dikes. "We're living between the Gays and the Dikes? " I said. "What are the odds of that happening?"

"You're not finished yet," my mother said. "You have the Furbushes across the street."

"What is this, some kind of a joke?" I said.

My father was already clutching his sides in hysteria. He's been known to erupt into uncontrollable fits of laughter. I saw him lose it several times when I was a child where he literally rolled around on the kitchen floor trying to catch his breath from maniacal chortling. At any rate, we were definitely not done yet.

We all got back in the car to see if our street was the only street with suggestive names. It certainly was not. The subdivision was a treasure trove of hilarious names. There were Willys. There were Hardons. There were Pastards (hopefully not mean-spirited ones with a vicious dog). And there were my personal favorites – the Peckers of Yonkers. And, more!

Can you imagine the dinner party? "Gays, I'd like you to meet the Dikes; Hardons, if you're not too intimidated by the Peckers of Yonkers, I'd like to introduce you to the Willys. Hey, you Pastards, you're invited but please leave your vicious dog at home. Check out the buffet, everyone. We have delicious weenies."

And, did I mention the Krapps? Seriously? What happens if you become friendly with people with a name like that and you want to go out for a bite? Where do you take a Krapp for dinner? I'm just wondering.

In the meantime, my father was rolling around in the backseat of our rental vehicle. He damn near knocked my mother out of the car. I was having my very own paroxysm in the passenger seat while my well-mannered husband was anxious to escape civilization and check out the marsh. He was giggling a little, though.

I think that might have been the last laugh my father ever had – I mean the side-clutching type. And, I was so glad to be there to share it with him. Dawson died in 2010 and my father followed suit on October 3, 2011. My mother still laughs about the Waverly incident.

We still own the property in Waverly. In fact, we visited the property (and Dawson and Pearl!) again in 2009. Unfortunately, we never got to meet our neighbors. They probably would have thought we were silly jackasses, anyway – no matter what we brought to the party.

ABOUT THE AUTHOR

Mindy Littman Holland is a writer, artist and photographer living in Santa Fe, New Mexico. In addition to *All My Funny Ones*, she is the author of *Wait Until You're Fifty: A Woman's Journey Into Midlife* and *The Rebirth of Gershon Polokov*, a novel. She has also created numerous drawing and photography books and designs wearable art. Her blog can be found on her website at www.mindylittmanholland.com.